The Divine Whispers

Songs of the Truth - Volume One

Mohammad Younus Koul

SELF PUBLISHED

The Divine Whispers - Songs of the Truth Volume One

by Mohammad Younus Koul

ISBN (paperback): 978-93-340-8745-1

Self-published by Mohammad Younus Koul
Srinagar, Jammu and Kashmir, India

Cover design by [Basit Wani]

In Loving Memory of my mother

Dear Mother,
It was not easy in that time,
being a woman in her prime,
Widowed at thirty-five years' age,
Not to go for second marriage,
Permitted by the Law of Islam,
But you were a mother outstanding.
You stopped drops of your bitter tears,
Your young husband and your youngest child
Drowned in the Dal Lake,
Your doctor son fled to a foreign country.
Despite these misfortunes, you did not give in,
Nothing could dampen down your resilience.
You were my defender and Salvatore.
Amidst all sorrow and sadness.
I love you, Mom! I love you, Mom!
My life is because of you,
I learnt great lessons from you,
You sacrificed yourself at the altar of your family,
For bringing up your orphaned children.
You made us engineers, doctors, and professors.
You gave up all your comforts and joys,
For our growth and development.
You are the one to whom I owe,
Every best thing that I own.
You got us out of darkness to light,
You gave us higher education.
You were the best manager and administrator,
You were a hard master too.
I love you, Mom! I love you, Mom!
The best Mom! An epitome of sacrifice!

Introduction

The Divine Whispers: Songs of the Truth is a profound collection of poetry by Mohammad Younus Koul that explores divine reality and spiritual awakening. Through lyrical verse, Koul delves into themes of love, enlightenment, and the eternal quest for truth, reflecting deep contemplation of the divine presence and drawing readers into a journey of inner discovery.

The poetry navigates the intricate relationship between the human soul and the divine, capturing moments of revelation and introspection. Koul's eloquent expressions highlight the beauty of the natural world and the omnipresence of the divine, inviting readers to perceive the sacred in everyday life.

The Divine Whispers serves as a spiritual guide, inspiring readers to reflect on their journey toward enlightenment and recognize divine manifestations around them. Through evocative and heartfelt verses, Koul brings to life the profound connection between the earthly and the eternal, making this collection a cherished companion for seekers of wisdom and truth.

Table of Contents

1 When Beauty Divine Upon the Eyes Rests

When beauty divine upon the eye's rests,
And grace divine cloaks body and soul bright,
My mind finds peace with what I hear and see,
With heart's eyes and ears, while gazing at night.
Within the silent realm of the heart's depth,
Lie yearnings blessed upon my ears and eyes.
O Allah! Shed thy blessings, rains of mercy,
For only wisdom can dispel these doubts,
That might hinder the path you wish for me,
To understand how love divine conquers,
Veiling from the One those deluded souls.
Neither whims nor force bring awareness clear
Of Absolute unity, profound truth.
Though body may wane with the passing time,
My love transcends this mortal veil always.
For in the darkness, my soul shines a star,
Where burdened hopes prevail and continue.
No blemish tarnishes what I perceive,
For love is seen only through purity.

2 *I did not take the human form of my own accord*

I did not take the human form of my own accord,
I was not asked for my willingness,
when I was to be born (as His vicegerent?).
Had I known that the life of this world
is nothing but the enjoyment of delusion,
I would not have wished to be born here;
this is, however, God's decision to test me.
I must not be contentious and argue with Him
about His sending me to this world;
just I must remind myself that
of His spirit He has blown into me.
He is the Most Gracious, the Most Merciful!
Without my asking,
He cares for me and blesses me with bounties;
I need not moan or mourn for anything.
I owe Him everything I have, He is my Lord!
I live just for and because of Him;
I'm fond of His beautiful music and light,
and all His self-manifestation
in the heavens and the earth
and all that He has created between them!

3 *In the Shadows of Your Mercy's Domain*

In the shadows of your mercy's domain,
Without requisitioning I get your immense love,
A silent exhibition of Divine Providence
I watch your manifestation, with a yearning gaze,
As your smile dances in the musical embrace.
Your sweet voice, a symphony to my ears,
Yet you remain beyond my senses' reach,
I offer my heart and soul to you, and you see,
My pure love that blooms so fiercely in me.
Like a flower in a desert, I stand alone,
Nurturing desire to be seen by you awaiting
A silent fire of love consumes my soul,
As mad moth sacrifices its life
Going round the flame
But still, I cherish the ardent hope
Of being reborn like a phoenix
Finding solace in your rhythmic dance.
For even in the depths of my afterlife mysteries,
I'll keep on loving you, as the Only-reality
Ignited on heart, my fire of love is pure,
A flame of love that forever shall endure.
In this silent story of love, I'll quietly stay,
Hoping one day I'll come to see One-reality.

4 *Oh, what a Great Awareness It Will Be*

Oh, what a Great Awareness it will Be;
To know Who I Am on All Aspects of ME.
The physical, the psychological, the spiritual!
What a Great Awareness it will be;
To Be Able to See Who I am? What is One-reality?
Oh, what a Great Awareness it will Be!
Having the illusion removed from the mind
Having the Blindfolds removed from the Vision;
We can see clearly into the gorgeous manifestation:
The Unity in diversity! The One-reality!
Oh, what a Great Enlightenment it will Be!
The World of Creation is the fantastic manifestation
Of Divine Energy;
Giving Birth To All The Things Comprising One-reality!
But the Flawed Vision of The Polytheists cannot
See into it One-reality;
Just ask yourself:
What kind of Knowledge is needed to know One-reality?
Divine Knowledge! Yes, that only can help you know One-reality
Divine Knowledge one cannot have in a Madrassa
Or from any person professing as a Spiritual Guru;
One can acquire such a knowledge with Divine Intellect only;
But, to be honest, 'Such is God's bounty!
He grants it to anyone who is willing [to receive it];
For God is limitless in His great bounty!'
Then, without any shame, we must ask Him

For granting us such a bounty;

Only the persons with Divine Intellect can have

Serenity and tranquility

Cause they comprehend One-reality;

Oh what a great Spiritual Awakening it will be!

When we Know: who I am and what is One-reality?

5 *One Day We Will See the Dawning of Eternal Peace*

One day we will see the dawning of eternal peace;
The ecstasy of tomorrow is but a gentle breeze;
That simply brushes off our face the dust of duality;
The thought of Tomorrow's joyful Eid puts us in tranquility.
We are in wilderness after losing the way to the Garden of eternity;
Rarely do we try to find the Wisdom flower, and the Knowledge tree;
Rarely do we lift our heads to wonder at the glory of one-reality;
Rarely do we remember our covenant with God
That We will be grateful to Him for His being our Lord!
Let us be Thankful to Him
In the light of day, and in the dark of night!
A chance to feel that we are born of His command Be!
We are born to sing His hymns and glorify His beauty!
Let us breathe the air of his music with joy and awe!
And be able to sail in our boat in the sea of one-reality!

6 *I Do Believe That the Day of Qiyamah Is Near*

I do believe that the Day of Qiyamah is near;
I do not believe that my death is sure;
I believe that my real being is not mortal;
When Izrael closes in on me
I will be alone to follow him;
But certainly with you I will be there
On the Day of resurrection;
I am happy, because I believe
You will only appear
On the Day of resurrection;
So I don't fear my demise!
After the current phase of life I will reappear! I am sure!
Just after my demise
I will come back to life;
The second phase of life! Resurrection!
Miraculous and marvelous event!
With divine eyes
Will I rise from the dead!
I will see your beauty with divine eyes;
I truly pray for divine eyes;
Please grant me those eyes
To allow me love your beauty;
Be I in Jannah or Jahannam
After the order of judgement

I will continue loving you

Gazing into your manifestation.

7 *Rising from the Dead*

Rising from the dead is in every way
Spectacular and miraculous;
Cause the dead have not to stay dead;
'And says man:
What! when I am dead
Shall I truly be brought forth alive?
Does not man remember
That We created him before,
When he was nothing?'
Until the Day of resurrection
No one will be raised from the dead;
Everything is bound to perish
Save His (eternal) Self!
To show all that they have to account
For their deeds and beliefs
With Him rests all judgement on that day
When one and all will be raised from the dead;
And unto Him shall we all be brought back!
By His permission
Israfil will blow the trumpet, and shout: Rise!
Rise by the command of my Lord!
In the same manner
When the Arifeen hear the trumpet
They wake up from the deep ignorance;
Their mind, soul, heart, their whole person
Revives and rises from the dead

In response to Divine call to know one-reality;
From the start of ages, sages have proclaimed:
La moujood illa hu - there exists only one-reality!
He who comprehends this truth of one-reality
For him this divine knowledge is Proof of Salvation!
Dead are only they who are drained of
Flow of divinely music and light;
They who recover from illusion
And disillusion can walk with divine!
Dualism begets the delusion
About the existence of one-reality.

1. Quran: 19: 66-67

8 *The Divinely Thoughts I Really Treasure*

The divinely thoughts I really treasure
I take every care to keep unpolluted
My thoughts are real and pure
My pleasure to have such a treasure.

9 *In the Depths of My Divine Self*

In the depths of my divine self - the fathomless ocean
Where attributes and being do coincide,
I pen these lines, heavy with wisdom,
Expressing my joy of finding you
Beyond comparison with or in contrast to anything!
Overwhelming is the warmth of your musical embrace
Leaving no space in me empty and desolate!
Filling up the void that I experienced before!
Everywhere your presence!
In the echoes of silence
I notice the existence of one-reality;
Each passing moment
A reminder anew, of your presence I listen;
Never absent in me or around!
My heart, a vessel, overflowing with honey sweet;
Overflowing with euphoria, no way I am missing you!
Like a phoenix bird with eternal wings
In ecstasy's symphony my spirit sings:
I am immortal!
I am reality!
I am the truth!
I am Absolute unity!
Yearning for satisfaction in the perpetual remembrance
The solace of your omnipresence, so enveloping I feel!
Without your all-time remembrance
The world seems to me colorless

And drained of light and music!

As I navigate the sights of your beautiful manifestation

Your laughter, your touch, your embrace my soul feels!

Lost in the depths of this heart-warming presence in one-reality

I cherish the sweet memory of my days in paradise;

No more now I want to tread

The labyrinthine streets and alleys of this mournful world;

Apprehension to lose the sight of omnipresence once more

Leaves my soul sore;

So let the joy of knowing one-reality

Flow out from my eyes!

Let my heart dance in ecstasy!

For in the manifestation of one-reality

Spiritual peace and solace I find

Because of being a staunch believer in one-reality.

10 The Fuel of My Love's Fire

The fuel of my love's fire! The divine energy!
Resonating music inside and outside,
strong yet tender tunes that don't stop!
Divine eyes see the truth of one reality—
a divine fire burning in the heart!
A hot passion makes my heartbeat faster and faster
because of the passionate desire in me
to hold you, to touch you, and to gaze into you.
But how can I hold you, touch you, and gaze into you?
Impossible! You do not have a corporeal body.
Let me then make a humble supplication:
Hold me, rather, in your musical arms;
touch me with your musical hands;
gaze at me with your musical eyes,
so that I am enveloped by your sweet music,
bringing awareness and enlightenment slowly in me—
that music is my reality,
that my Lord has blown into me.

11 The Music of the La Illaha Illa Hu

The music of the ***La illaha illa hu***

Sings in my heart

And also resonates in Afaq

A spiritual awakening and enlightenment:

Nothing is there except one-reality!

The voice comes from the unseen

Not from man-made flute or lute!

You can feel with the divine intellect:

The Absolute Reality is the hidden secret!

When my ears and eyes hear

The holy voice echoing

I feel it is sprouting from every atom!

What this holy voice is revealing?

The Surah al-ikhlas in sweet musical tunes!

'He is the One God:

God the Eternal!

The Uncaused Cause of All Being!

He begets not,

And neither is He begotten!

He is unique! Incomparable!

'God is one-reality!'

The pleasing voice comes from the depth of my being!

I affirm my Lord is one-reality

Without seeing!

When Words fail me

To explain this truth

The music speaks for me!

My divine vision sees one-reality!

Which my physical eyes cannot see!

12 *Divine Word Is Just a Connector to Divine*

Divine word is just a connector to divine
It is not an end in itself
But a means to an end: the divine pleasure;
The wise and awakened lovers listen closely
To the word divine with the heart's ear;
God showers the choicest blessings upon his friends
Who constantly listen to the divine word;
And in no time the listeners of divine word
Get at peace with their self and with other children of God
And above every blessing they attain Divine pleasure;
Their reward [awaits them] with God:
Gardens of perpetual bliss!
Through which running waters flow!
Therein to abide beyond the count of time!
Well-pleased is God with them!
And well-pleased are they with Him:
All this awaits him who of his Sustainer
Stands in awe!
This is the good news told by God to his friends in Qur'an!

13 *He Talks to Me in Silence*

He talks to me in silence, but in a wordless voice;
He speaks to me close by in my ears and through my eyes;
I do not see him in any physical form any time anywhere;
He is away from the reach of the senses five;
Explore the skies and the earth, you will not find him there;
Searching him at any place is a gross error!
Even so all the while I am immersed in his thoughts;
Be I sleeping or awake! Be it day or night!
I am feeling the burning heat of the sun of his love on my heart;
Hearing incessantly a lovely melody emanating as if from the heavens;
Perhaps it is a sign from the Almighty that He loves me immensely;
Who is this Almighty constantly calling me?
Why should the Almighty call me?
Drowning in the river of divine symphony for so many years
I have wondered the difference between the listener and the caller;
All the same, through this melody I feel connected to Almighty
As I remember the command given to me
Through the medium of the Qur'an:
Yaaa aiyuhal lazeena aamanut taqul laaha
Wabtaghooo ilaihil waseelata
Wa jaahidoo fee sabeelihee la'allakum tuflihoon;
'O YOU who have attained to faith!
Remain conscious of God;
And seek wasilah to come closer unto Him;
And strive hard in His cause;

So that you might attain to a happy state;
I hear this verse as if an angel is reciting
This verse to me in the angelic voice.

14 There Is No I and There Is No You

There is no I and there is no You!
How can there be union or separation?
What sense is there in trying to see him
By meditation, or by renunciation?
But rather, directly know the reality
That He is whole!
Nothing can be included in him!
Nothing can be excluded from him!
He is absolutely one-reality
Perfect and whole!
He is as He was!
He will be as He is!
From beginning to end, He is unchangeable!
That we fail to comprehend one-reality
Is because in fact we are under illusion;
We wrongly perceive our false identities
As being separate realities.

15 *Before He Thought of Manifestation*

Before He thought of manifestation
His beauty, which now is reflected
In the mirror-house of the world of creation
Was like a treasure buried under soil;
Or He was like a beautiful bride
Fully covered under black chador;
So His glory was never witnessed!
A diamond hidden in the rock!
Then, He created human with divine eyes;
Only then could He be known!
Thus, He saw himself by himself
Through the human eyes;
As the verse of the Qur'an mentions:
Laa tudrikuhul absaaru
Wa Huwa yudrikul absaara
Wa huwal Lateeful Khabeer!
('No vision can grasp Him,
But His grasp is over all vision:
He is above all comprehension
Yet is acquainted with all things.')

16 *I Have My Own Book of Knowledge*

I have my own book of knowledge!
Don't teach me anymore
Your lessons that teach duality;
I don't want to know
What God does not inspire me;
I believe in one divinely source;
Knowledge and wisdom drops
Trickle down on my heart
About one reality constantly;
And unfold the secrets untold;
My beliefs are pure and divine!

17 Through the Wended Ways We Are Dawdling

Through the wended ways we are dawdling;
Seeking knowledge from the dead books and the dead gurus!
We are stuffed with obnoxious ideas and beliefs
And perform thoughtless exercises of meditation;
That weigh us down and render us unable
To scale the heights and achieve the feats;
But, he who is gifted with divine intellect
Makes amends silently to his flawed beliefs;
The beliefs that dupe us into believing
That the simulated sunrises
And smog-infested skies are reality!
These illusions give us only twisted meanings
That have little semblance to reality;
Our blurred vision stops us from clearly seeing
In the ever-changing manifestation, the one-reality;
It's awfully funny how people assume an illusion to be a reality;
They judge a book by its cover
And read not the whole book between the lines;
Believe me!
The reality is explained in the pages of the Book of manifestation;
The sages read through this book to get to know
The attributes of one-reality!

18 *Accepting the Existence of One-Reality*

Accepting the existence of one-reality is the real obedience to God;
The obedience to God is not just to perform the man-made rituals
Or to follow the dogmas and doctrines preached
By the obscurantist and extravagantly orthodox Sufis or Mulla's;
The obedience to God is to acquire the prophetic wisdom and knowledge of one-reality;
There is nothing for me to surrender
But my undivine knowledge that I learnt
From ignorant and illusioned Sufis and Mulla's;
The obedience to God is to give up false teaching
Of deifying, dead or living, Sufis and Mulla's;
I surrender to nothing but to the thoughts
That come to me about the existence of one-reality;
My surrendering to my thoughts is because these are
Inspirations from my God;
There is to me no religion apart from the inspiration
About the existence of one-reality;
I cannot surrender to duality and idolatry in any form!
Pity the person who does not have in his heart
The certainty about the existence of one-reality.

19 *You Are Away*

You are away, far away, roaming in the valleys of illusion;
Come, come, come near to one-reality;
So far away lost in wilderness
You cannot see the overwhelming one-reality;
Come, come, come near to one-reality;
Turn, turn back! Gently come out of illusion of duality;
Together the whole manifestation in the multiverse
Comprises one-reality;
Apart from one-reality, I know not of anything in the multiverse
Being in itself a distinct and separate reality;
In my essence too, I am not distant from one-reality;
When I contemplate on the essence of my own existence
I see I am neither away nor near to one-reality;
I am not a dualist suffering from blurred vision;
I believe solely and wholly in the existence of One-reality!
What is one reality?
Fas'alooo ahlaz zikri in kuntum laa ta'lamoon!
(Ask the people of knowledge, if you do not know!)

20 *The Awakened Soul*

The awakened soul

A shadow fallen into a river of music

Turning carefully against the pressure of a spirit from within

The vile beguiling nafs

Flowing towards the fathomless sea where the heart

Breathes

For the expected calm

Of when we

Realize our essential reality

The all- encompassing One-reality.

21 *Do Not Be Stuck in a Void*

Do not be stuck in a void
And detached from the manifestation of one-reality;
Do not think yourself to be alone
Separate and cut off from one-reality;
I am scared that if you follow the religion of duality
You will forget about your home of eternity
Where you lived in peace and tranquility;
I am afraid that if you do not gain awareness of one-reality
You will go through motions of illusion and disillusion constantly;
You will be visited all the time by disturbing
Routine thoughts and feelings of separation and duality;
You will not feel yourself to be the real pearl anymore
And will just be like an empty shell without the pearl inside;
If you do not realize the existence of one-reality
Your mind will become your own personal hell
In which you will suffer forever, and God will tell you:
'The Fire be your dwelling-place:
You will dwell therein forever, except as Allah willeth;
For thy Lord is full of wisdom and knowledge'

22 I Aspire of a Life When I Would Be Free

I aspire of a life when I would be free like a rock pigeon!
My mind has turned me into a pet pigeon - a prisoner of nafs!
Since the hour I came down on earth by my Lord's command
Most of my days have been trampled by illusion and disillusion;
Life of a person who has lost his way in the wilderness
Of the world really doesn't excite me anymore!
I have been rebelling against my True self
And befriending the vile nafs!
Now by the grace of my Lord this friendship might forever come to an end;
I will inshallah get free of struggling everyday
Just to keep myself away from following the Satan;
Just because I am keeping in mind the verse reminding me of my covenant with my Lord:
'Alam a'had ilaykum yaa Baneee Aadama al-laa ta'budush-Shaytaana
Innooo lakum aduwwum mubeen'
(Did I not enjoin on you, O you children of Adam, that you should not worship Satan
Since, verily, he is your open foe)
Now I know what a great bliss it is to be
So engrossed in the perennial remembrance of my Lord.

23 *Before That Your Hair Turn Grey*

Before that your hair turn grey
And you reach the worst of your age
Before that you lose your patience to face
All your inner and outer conflicts
It is a time of remembering who you truly are;
It is a time of aligning with what is the one-reality;
What you are here to do
And what you are here to be;
A time of really letting go the things
That do not serve your real purpose in this life;
A time of really doing what you have promised
To God in pre eternity;
A time of surrendering wholly to the will of God!
And feeling the abundance of truth
The abundance of the real sunlight shining
Softly on your mind, soul, and heart;
Feeling of integration with the beautiful manifestation of God;
So let you feel:
The abundance of the birds chirping!
For us to hear them sing in the morning and evening;
The abundance of the trees growing!
For us to look at and take in the Oxygen
The abundance of the water flowing!
For us to drink, take bath, and irrigate;
The abundance of fresh fruits and vegetables!
For us as food and to taste

A little bit of heaven within;

He has created the sun, the moon, and the galaxies of stars for you;

He has spread out the earth for all creatures;

In which there are fruits and date palms with spathes;

And grains with leafy stems, and fragrant plants;

Let us open all our senses that God has gifted us

To enjoy the beauties of his manifestation;

So don't forget to say:

Which, then, of your Sustainer's powers can you disavow?

24 It Is So Difficult for Me to Tell What I Hear

It is so difficult for me to tell what I hear;
I wish I could utter it in words, but I can't;
Just no words for the tunes of the unstrung harp!
But only infinitely long sweet sound of Hu;
If this divine music ever stopped
Time would come to a halt;
I would stop living in zikrullah (remembering divine)
If I do not listen to this eternal music in my heart;
Lord's name Hu resonates all the time in me
Like a delicate breeze creating resonation
As it passes through the green foliage of trees;
Putting a listener's heart at rest and in peace;
It flows with grace like a roaring mountain river
Enchanting heart and soul,
Listening to this Isme Azam (the greatest name)
My heart pulsates fast
With a view to aligning with the sound of Hu;
Creating, as a result, a symphony of love, peace, and tranquility
That never ends.

25 *You Are the Ocean*

You are the ocean,
I am the running water;
I flow from You to You,
In a circular motion!
I am an eye,
You are the beauty;
I look from You to You!
You are not my body;
You are not my soul;
You are the whole;
I am not cut off from You!
I am a traveler;
You are my guide;
I travel from You to You!

26 Meeting the Real Is Beyond Every Fantasy

Meeting the real is beyond every fantasy!
Wear on your eyes Love of one-reality!
Leaving the absurdity of visioning duality!
Walk with the real when you're walking
In the garden of the manifest-reality;
Over you will sweep waves of one-reality;
And soothe your soul with the cool of one-reality;
Let your mind expire and divine intellect replace
So that you find the way to one-reality;
Unfolding the hidden meanings of the verses
That are in a well-guarded divine book of reality;
None but the pure [of heart] can know one-reality;
Be patient! In your own time shall open to you one-reality;
Reading the secrets in your soul's rhythm
Will make you dance with Divine in ecstasy;
And in the universe, you will feel presence of one-reality;
Clear the jaded memories from your past
When you indulged in the practice of duality;
Steer clear out of the mire of this duality!
Then only can you clear the confusions of the past;
Mysteries are too hard to understand for you
As long as you are unaware of and unenlightened about
The existence of one-reality;
Perceiving one-reality as the core of manifestation

More and more creates the yearn for loving one-reality;

Dualists flock like a moth to a flame and enter

The Womb of illusion and disillusion!

They can never comprehend the secret of one-reality.

27 *Look into the Beautiful Manifestation*

LOOK - look into the beautiful manifestation!
For if you don't look,
You will fail to see divine
Well-camouflaged around;
When given the mirror before you
Don't look aside and ask for the glimpse
Look - look into the mirror and see
Who is reflected there?
He is not in Heavens afar!
Look - look into the mirror and see
Who is standing independently tall and high before you;
Then you came, then I loved you more than what I could ever have.
Look - look into the mirror and see whom you unintentionally denied,
Whom you thought had never been there before;
I looked into the mirror and I saw the image;
I bowed to the image in the mirror
I admit that seeing him in the mirror is possible but seeing him out of mirror is indeed impossible.
I lost myself into the mirror,
The ego that I manned vanished;
When I am with you, I realize
I am nothing but you are the only reality
I'm writing this poem here,
And the beauty is for thee to see

I had known for it to be only a glimpse
But ultimately, eventually, when I disappeared as an onlooker it struck me that I see myself in the mirror
This wonderful thought gravitated me deep down to reality.
So thank you, O mirror, undeniably you have shown me my lord. I love you, o mirror of my lord.

28 *When Love Is Divine*

When love is divine,
You will never beg for luxurious way of life;
When love is divine,
You will feel vast sea of love deep in your soul;
When love is divine,
You will feel echoing in your heart the sweet music divine;
When love is divine,
You will receive the green light of the Lamp divine;
When love is divine,
You will not fall prey to the schemes of the villain Satan;
When love is divine,
Both your nafs and heart will submit to you together;
When love is divine,
You will easily come out of illusion and delusion of mind;
When love is divine,
You will be gifted with profound awareness and enlightenment;
When love is divine,
You will be blessed with wisdom and knowledge divine;
When love is divine,
You will find in self and the universe one-reality;
When love is divine,
You will comprehend that your true self is from one-reality;
When love is divine,
You will have an innate urge to keep on loving one-reality;
When love is divine,
You will surely grasp with divine intellect the truth of one-reality;

When love is not divine,

You will go astray from the prophetic way;

You will not be conscious of your divinely reality!

29 *In the Depths of My Heart*

In the depths of my heart
A music I wish to constantly listen;
One that's never been heard!
A pure diamond, unbroken!
The eternal music of paradise!
The rhythm that joins to the eternal reality!
The melody that sings the word of God!
The music that brings divinely message
That from the heavens comes down!
The music with tunes that flow like a river!
The music that produces emotions fair;
The music that makes the listener a whirling dervish!
The ancient music that captures the soul!
The music heard on the Day of Alast!
When God told: Am I not Your Lord?
And boldly we had said: Yes, our Lord!
The music that leaves listeners feeling whole!
The music that makes realize one-reality!
The music that speaks of love and life!
The music that gives all the joys and removes strife!
The music that generates light that never fades!
The music that helps listeners have dreams sweet!
The music that is one of a divine kind!
The music that is a true treasure to find!
The music that makes see the enduring beauty!
The music forever pure, holy, and true beauty!

30 I Promise You That You Will Win When You Stop Crying

I promise you that you will win when you stop crying!
I promise you that you will fail when you stop trying!
I promise you that you will be happy when you stop fearing!
I promise you that you will be sad when you stop hoping!

31 Hey Reality, I Know I Am Ignorant of You

Hey Reality, I know I am ignorant of you;
I won't pretend to know you absolutely;
But I try to know myself and not in vain;
I take a deep breath, finding around me one-reality;
Let me think and talk about your beauty;
Let me take a bold view of your manifestation
And find a way of loving you exclusively;
With me self-annihilated in your reality
I find nothing exists except you;
The obstacle in the way of understanding one-reality
Is my past learning that there actually exists duality;
So please, O one-reality - don't let me suffer
In the delusion of duality;
For brave is a choice to be made about
Accepting the religion of one-reality;
Only the pure lovers of Absolute Unity
Can such a brave choice make;
As by joining the elite people professing
The religion of Absolute Unity
My heart can bloom like a lotus flower
That out of water cannot bloom;
Know, my friends, that I am here to listen
With an open heart and keen ear
To the song of one-reality;

With it my soul's ecstasy starts to increase boundlessly;
Let all of us together celebrate without fear
The perennial spring of one-reality.

32 Stumbling, Slipping Down into the Gorge of Hell

Stumbling, slipping down into the gorge of hell;
The sinners' bones are broken and crushed
By the weight of peace lessness and unhappiness;
Their screams from torment and terror echo in my ears;
Making me filled with awful dread
As I think of my own fate after this life;
My own screams, groaning and moaning
With horrible pain I couldn't hear;
It is a horrible sight of The Hell to see!
The transgressor's destination!
The day is sure to come
When the hair of children with fear will turn grey!
So let me find a way back to my lord!
Let me take a back turn and start
Walking on Unity's Way:
No infidelity!
No blind faith!
No meaningless rituals!
No meditational exercises!
Only one step needed to take on the path of love:
Let me withdraw myself away from myself!
This Path of love is straight and the shortest!
I must choose this road of Divine Love, and
Then sit in the thought and remembrance of one-reality!

All the dread of chastisement in the burning Hell
Instantly will go!
Verily the Hell is your own self!
Behold! When your self annihilates
Only one-reality remains!
That is the true paradise!

33 *When a Person in Deep Slumber*

When a person in deep slumber,
hears in the early hours,
The Muazzin calling to come to the Lord:
The meeting with the Lord is better than the sweet deep sleep!
The person hearing the call is free
Either to declare the great Yes or the great No
To the Caller's call!
The person who is bold to say the Yes
The believer within him is awakened and enlightened!
He is saying to His God:
'Our Lord! We have heard the caller to true belief
Proclaiming come to God! We believe in you alone!
Our Lord! Forgive our sins! Absolve us of our misdeeds!
And allow us to die as one of the virtuous persons!'
Such a believer is elevated by the Lord
From honor to honor!
He is strong in his conviction! He is strong in his belief!
The person who refuses and does not repent
For his sins and misdeeds
And in his arrogance says No to the caller's call
While still sleeping under the quilt
Within him is a rejecter residing;
Who drags him down all his life into:
Ignorance, illusion, and delusion!
Such a person if desists not, God shall most surely
Drag him down upon his forehead!

On the Day, when he is dragged to the hell fire

He shall say:

"Oh would that I were utter dust!"

34 *We Cannot Ignore It*

We cannot ignore it,
Learn and listen to the nafs-e-lawama within;
Spiritual peace is the invaluable thing we must achieve;
Yet it grows bigger and bigger like the sun's light after dawn;
It is the real thing that gives divinely meaning to our life;
And as such we must be constantly in its search;
Spiritual peace! That leads to real salvation;
If you desire to achieve spiritual peace
You can cultivate it only in its proper place;
Our turbulence-free and equanimous heart is the proper place!
Spiritual peace is our ace, it is the mother of world peace;
To make a candid confession
We are continually destroying our spiritual peace;
So, in the end, we have to admit our defeat in finding the peace;
We become childish in this world to have cheap fun
And then at the end of the day we find, we are done;
Frustrated and dejected as we get
We dread at the end of lifetime of an unpeaceful afterlife;
When we realize that we have failed to achieve the spiritual peace;
Our hungry glutton nafs feasts on our spiritual peace!
It happens too often until it leads us to our grave
Without having achieved the spiritual peace;
In that moment, grieving and praying
For the Eternal Peace is but in vain;
Well, let you fight your nafs now before you are put in the coffin;
This nafs is your dreadful enemy residing deep inside you;

Fight it out from your heart so that you could find your spiritual peace.

35 *I Know It Is Right for Me*

I know it is right for me
To spend my time with lovers
Who truly love one-reality;
I just don't want to associate myself
With people who believe in duality:
Whether it's the Mulla giving sermons on the pulpit
Or the philosophers who couldn't see one-reality!
I consider myself to be like a flute
In the hands of a flute player
Who controls the kind of tunes the flute should produce;
Cause there prevails absolutely one-reality!
It's the one-reality who is in himself
Command, commander, and commanded in this world of creation;
Who himself makes plans and programs
For the manifestation of his powers of creation;
He is one-in-all and all-in-one reality!
Look at the sun, the moon, the galaxies of stars
Hewanaat, jamadaat, and nabataat
And different things in the multiverse
All of them are manifestations of one-reality!
Say goodbye to duality so that
We will see each other not as separate but as one-reality, one-humanity!

36 *When Your Beauty Holds Me Captive*

When your beauty holds me captive
I can feel the power of your immense love;
I feel an irresistible impulse in me to see you
Through the veils on your beautiful face;
I believe that you are secretly peeping
Through these veils at your lovers;
I believe that it is only you around me
When I vision Your beautiful manifestation surrounding me,
I believe it is only you kissing my forehead
When the cool breeze in your garden touches me;
When I see your light flashes touching me
The feeling of ecstasy is electrifying me;
I express my intense love for you
Through loving the things in the world of your creation;
There is no denying this reality!
When I behold your beautiful creation
I can feel your great magnetic power
That in every moment attracts me towards your beauty;
I feel I am the happiest person that I've ever been
When I feel that you are glancing at me; EVER
I do feel that I am nothing
But the lover of your manifestation, EVER!

37 *Strive to Discover Now the Mystery of One-Reality*

Strive to discover now the mystery of one-reality
Before this phase of life comes to its natural end;
If in present phase of life
You fail to know the meaning of one-reality
How will you then comprehend the secret
Of your existence now, and in next phase of life?
All that is revealed to you by divine intuition in wordless voice
It is for you to present that in a spoken language;
You must choose with care appropriate words
To weave the meanings of the revealed secrets and the wisdom pearls
Into the golden fabric of mystical poems.

38 Those Who Have Not Realized One-Reality Will Wander

Those who have not realized one-reality will wander:
Clueless in the present-life!
Aimless in the next-life!
Watch the lovers who have realized one-reality!
They dance with divine ecstasy
Grooving to the holy music night and day!
They merge into the music of one-reality!
They are free from the illusion of duality!
If you don't nurture in your heart
Love for knowing one-reality
The springs of knowledge and wisdom
Will not sprout in your heart;
You will live a life full with confusion
And will have delusion about reality.

39 *Look into the Manifestation*

Look into the manifestation!

Catch a glimpse by your divine eye

Of the being sitting inside!

Whispering your name in your ear:

Stand still and hear in my glorious voice:

'I am your reality!

I am one-reality!'

40 When You Contemplate with Your Divine Eye

When you contemplate with your divine eye:
All things in their essence are alike
You will see!
Little intrinsic differentiation
In the manifestation of all hues
You will see!
Just keep on coolly grooving to divine music:
All things are singing of one-reality
You will see!
Divinely beautiful manifestation, night and day
You will see!
Charming and in bloom all flowers of manifestation
You will see!
Sunshine as jewels, dew as divine pearls upon earth
You will see!
The fields gleaming golden, blessed by Sun and invigorated by the rain
You will see!
Streams of divine music flowing from Heavens
You will see!
In all this beautiful manifestation, one-reality
You will see!

41 Without Ever Having Known One-Reality

Without ever having known one-reality
All my poetry would have been such a waste
Of well worded time and effort;
But then, between myself and the one-reality
Who could ever guess
That there is no distance between;
The one reality loves me beyond any conceivable measure!
I am not too scared to proclaim
That one reality is rather undifferentiated and absolute!
It is naive to think that
One-reality is made of parts and components;
So I am left with a mystic feeling in my heart:
I am not a mere shadow of one reality!
I am a manifestation of one-reality!
I am not a broken or a separate component!
I am not concealed in a hollow husk
Like a grain!
I am not a poem incomplete!
I am not like a poem
Under construction in my heart
Waiting for its final touch.

42 Coming This Phase of Life to a Natural End

Coming this phase of life to a natural end
Our new phase of life in the next world starts;
There too possibly we will go with present-life mind;
After-life mind will just be
An extension of present-life mind;
So if you want to be happy there
Set your mind right here
Under the prophetic guidance;
It is then we shall find the real meaning of
What the sages of all epochs said:
'As you sow (here), so shall you reap (there)';
The death explains to us the book of life
That we have written with our pen;
When gone from this world
After we have breathed our last
Many of the present life beliefs
Will be proved wrong, far from reality, in after life;
There we shall realize, but in vain
How foolishly, naively we had clung
To myths and gods that never
Guided us to know one-reality.

43 *Do Not Grieve at My Grave to Mourn*

Do not grieve at my grave to mourn;
Why mourn my death when I'm just here?
You might not recognize me because
You are unaware of ever living one reality;
Instead, show persistence in loving the manifestation of one-reality;
See Me blooming in the rose garden of manifestation!
Enrich yourself with divine knowledge
In order to see the perennial existence of one-reality;
Listen! The one-reality never perishes with death!
But rather refreshes with new and newer appearances
In its rose garden of manifestation!

44 *To Man, I Know Not of a Face*

To Man, I know not of a face
More beautiful than yours;
To the divine music,
I know not of a sound
More sweet than you;
To the divine light,
I know not of a light
More bright than you;
To death,
I know not of an event
More certain like you;
To life,
You are all I know
The truth! The reality! Life!
I know not of any sign of one-reality
More manifest than you;
To man,
I know not of any being
More in the image of God than you!
Man!
You are the divine secret! Divine is your secret!

45 I Am Amazed by the Omnipresence of One-Reality in

I am amazed by the omnipresence of One-reality in:
Mountains high, oceans wide, verdant forests
Beautiful moors, and meadows with blooming flowers;
Sweet springs, gushing mountain streams, and majestic rivers
Flowing continually, calmly and quietly towards the seas;
And different living creatures - small and big -
That in this universe reside;
As I with my divine eye view this beautiful sight
I cannot help but feel that I am the integral part of one-reality;
Because the unparalleled beauty of the one-reality is manifest in the whole creation;
We must not differentiate between one thing and the other
In this world of marvelous and graceful manifestation;
I hold in my mystical embrace the beautiful one-reality
And cherish, love, and glorify the grace of one-reality;
I see with my divine intellect that only one-reality
Flourishes in me and out of me;
Let us take a solemn pledge:
We will, in no case, accept and follow the religion of duality;
Let us pledge to our creator:
We will never doubt the existence of one-reality;
Let us pledge to our Lord:
We will not ascribe partners to one-reality;
So that we can continue to nurture our soul

With the light and music of divinity;
For if we fail in fulfilling our covenant with our Lord
We will fail to understand the Essence of one-reality.

46 I Never Stop to Wonder about One-Reality

I never stop to wonder about one-reality!
I never stop to think of one-reality!
I never stop to guess about one-reality!
I never even stop to notice one-reality!
There is someone in the background playing
Flute, lute, guitar, rabab and sitar;
While I get up,
I see in multivarious dresses manifest one-reality;
I never even once consider or see any reason
In deeming myself apart or other than one-reality;
Why?
Because I see both me and the whole manifestation
Praising and bowing down to one-reality;
I see beneath every pretty dress smiling
The brilliant face of one-reality;
I see in all seasons blooming
The colorful fragrant flowers of one-reality;
I see perfect, spotless - without faults
All around the awe-inspiring beauty of one-reality;
So pray tell me, my friends!
Do you also see the omnipresence of one-reality?
I dare to ask this personal question to you because
I see that almost whole population is deprived of
Noticing in the whole creation, one-reality.

47 *I Am Always with One-Reality, by Day and by Night*

I am always with one-reality, by day and by night;
I can feel the perennial presence of one-reality;
I can smell the perennial presence of one-reality;
I can hear the perennial music of one-reality;
In the cold night,
I feel the warmth of the presence of one-reality:
The heat rising from the burning flames
Of my love for one-reality!
Kindled from my burning passion for embracing one-reality!
When I go to sleep after day's toilsome work
The one-reality is present already there;
When I wake up from my sleep
The one-reality is already there:
In soft milk white morning light!
And in the cool morning breeze
Laden with the fragrance of one-reality;
Be it day or night, I cannot be without
The light and music of one-reality;
Sometime when I get lost in the wilderness
Of forgetfulness and ignorance
The one-reality in a flash of light appears before me
Like a father Kissing a prodigal son
On his coming back home;
The one-reality holds me tight to chest all the time

Whispering to me confidently in my heart's ear:

I will not lose you to the illusion or delusion of duality!

48 Someone Playing the Flute behind the Closed Door

Someone playing the flute behind the closed door;
It's sweet, getting sweeter, more and more;
I head to the door of my heart to hear
The sound of flute in its close range;
Curiosity leads me there to see
Who is playing behind the closed door?
I look through my divine eye - the window of my heart!
There is no one inside there!
Someone keeps playing the flute
Behind the closed door;
It resonates, and resonates more and more;
I sit outside the closed door enjoying the flute sound;
Expectation: the insider will sometime open the door;
Suddenly, the lights started flashing
Through the closed blinds;
I got free from the darkness overlapping me;
Everything became visible to my divine eye!
I saw the house is without doors and windows!
No insider there! No outsider there!
There is only one-reality!
I feel, I believe now, I am myself both
The player and hearer of the flute;
In comes awareness and enlightenment!
Out goes illusion and delusion!

49 To Sweet Celestial Tunes I've Given My Heart

To sweet celestial tunes I've given my heart;
To holy words that refresh I've given my heart;
To the book of divine knowledge I've given my heart;
To the shining pearls of wisdom I've given my heart.
Veiled was the face of the queen of my heart;
Her light passing through her veils
Illumined my heart;
O seekers of divine light!
This lamp of light I've found
In the niche of my heart.
Water of life is the soul that is blown into me;
Without body-frame soul can never activate;
The integration of body and soul is needed
To sustain the life in man.
The sweet melodious speech
My soul constantly hears
In the house of heart;
This sweet speech works as balm
For my sickness of love;
The speech resonates deep in my heart
The safe abode for soul!

50 The Central Figure of the World of Manifestation Is Man

The central figure of the world of manifestation is Man;
In arrogance, he who does not bow to Man
The fate of Iblis will meet that man;
Humiliated and disgraced will be that blind man!
The secret of the Divine manifestation truly is Man!
Using your Divine intellect, go and scan;
When God desired to manifest his powers
With His command Be, he created Man;
He set a seal of vicegerency upon the forehead of Man!
He would have not created the universe
Had he not to create Man;
(His Khalifa on the earth is Man!)
The sun and the moon and all the planetary bodies
Rotate and revolve for Man!
To tell you the truth
The mirror of God is the face of Man!
See the sovereign grace in the face of Man!
The pearl of divine reality is in the soul of Man!
The West and the East would not hear the message of God
If his mouthpiece were not Man;
Where is the lover who aspires to see God?
Let him come and know the secret of Man!
Divine is verily the reality of Man!
And he who does not perceive

The reality divine in Man:

He listens not the divine music of Man!

He understands not the reality of Man!

They are only like cattle!

No, more than that!

They are astray from the Right Path!

51 *Listen, the Wise Is the Sower Who Sows*

Listen, the wise is the Sower who sows
The seed in a fertile land;
But, lucky is the seed that the soil hides under it;
Unlucky is the seed that is sown in
A rocky and infertile soil or
Which the soil covers not, because;
Heat and cold will kill it!
Rains will wash it away!
Birds and insects will eat it away!
It dies, for it does not take roots in the soil;
Only the seeds sown in a good soil
Produce a good crop!
Likewise, your master gives to you a mystic seed
To be grown as the plant of mystic knowledge;
Take good care of it - as much as a good farmer does;
You will get million heads from a single seed!
Seed of spirituality grows perfectly well
Under the protective cover of Secrecy!
So said my master, Faqir M Rajab Guna to me!

52 *Man! Your Ears to Sweet Music Listen*

Man! Your ears to sweet music listen;
Yourself to virgin Horis of paradise listen;
Your divine eye to the divine beauty sees;
Your divine intellect the one-reality comprehends.
Man!
The beautiful reality has cast down the veils;
What lies there to discover for you?
Look into the core of manifestation!
The resplendent reality is smiling to you!
Man!
Acknowledge the presence of one-reality!
Study well the core reality of all manifestations!
You will notice omnipresent is the one-reality;
No blind, deaf, or mute can see but
The one-reality in the gorgeous manifestation.
Man!
The reality you can even discern
From the eye between your two brows;
Man!
Your moon-face with black archlike brows
Is the sign of one-reality;
Your teeth more precious than the Laa'l-e-Badakhshan
Are the sign of one-reality;
Man!
The ever sprouting spring under your tongue
(Sweet like Kawthar)

Is the sign of one-reality;

Man!

The quiver full of arrows - your eye-lashes

Is the sign of one-reality

Man!

Your eyes drunk with Love wine

Are the sign of one-reality

Man!

Your face, with light upon light

Is the sign of one-reality

Man!

Behold everything in the manifestation

Is the divine mirror;

Behold in it the beauty of one-reality!

55 In The Divine Eyes, A Spark Ignites

In the divine eyes, a spark ignites,
A flame that burns so pure and bright.
In divine touch, my heart takes flight,
In divine presence, I see my true light.
Divine whispers soft in midnight's hue,
Each whisper a promise, fresh and new.
Each whisper, new knowledge, and wisdom
In the divine glow, the essence is revealed.
In the dawn's smile, you greet the day,
Guiding me through life's twisting maze.
In the divine sun's warm embrace,
Love's sacred light illuminates my space.
No storm can dim this sacred divine light,
In its glow, I find endless delight.
In our essence, we are all together.
Living by dint of divine light.

56 God Is the Light of the Heavens and the Earth

God is the light of the heavens and the earth,
Light upon Light!
This Light encompasses all the worlds of manifestation!
But no eye can in any measure reach,
The reality of this Light!
The real is omnipresent though,
No human eyes can or have ever compassed Him!
He is the commander real and manifests himself through his command,
Be! And It Becomes!
Be silent!
Because no commentary in any scripture,
Can encompass His reality;
Only a skeptical person can say:
Is He or Is He not!
How is He? Where is He?
Through doubt and surmise no one can know,
The Truth and the Reality;
The man whose divine intellect perceives the reality,
Knows well that doubt and surmise cannot,
Encompass the divine reality;
With due regard to His being formless and indeterminate,
Bear this reality in mind,
That He alone is manifest in all things of manifestation;

No body in the worlds can exist without a soul,
And the Soul is nothing but His command Be!
The real—before manifestation—was The Hidden Treasure;
Open your divine eyes and see,
The Treasure is in your mine;
Although I am a finite body,
Boundless sea I can see through a minimalist camera,
That is fixed in my eyes;
My name is Adam! I am the noblest of all creatures!
On Mount of Mercy I reunited with my mate, Eve;
Here on this mountain we were forgiven our sins,
And our wilderness ended;
It is on this Mountain that the Prophet Muhammad stood and delivered,
The Farewell Sermon to his Companions;
A Manifesto for humankind!
Hold your tongue and silent be!
There is no other tongue that can deliver such a great sermon;
If you want to know what the reality is,
Know it from this Great prophet!

57 *Dream: The Fortified Town*

Dream:
The Fortified town:
All gates closed
I learned the inside way
From the insider
Calling from behind the veils:
Come in, come in:
Don't be scared
Don't loiter around
In wilderness!
Come Inside:
SPLENDOR
Cups of wine of love.
The saki:
Drink, drink!
If you are not
Ashamed of aspiring
To get in
Why are you ashamed
Of drinking the wine
In this tavern of love?
And he hugged me
With His arms of music
So close! So tight!
SAKI/ME
I am perplexed

Are both of us one

Or one disguised as two?

NO WITNESS

NO OTHER OBJECT IN SIGHT

I am myself

My own witness

NO SAKI

NO Wine

NO CUP

58 *I Take the Command from My Lord*

I take the command from my Lord,
His real servant I am;
The words of wisdom and the Qur'an,
Do I receive from God;
I am the one who was told by God,
The secret knowledge about things,
That even the angels did not know;
I am one who was made His Khalifa by God,
And to whom all the angels were bid to prostrate;
I am the one whom Nimrod threw into the bright blazing fire;
I am the one who was saved by God from Pharaoh,
The mighty but the cruel and vindictive king;
I am the one who was baptized by the water of life,
The enemies could not crucify or kill me;
I am the one who was blown into by God,
Of His spirit of immortality;
I am the one whose existence was caused by God,
The source of life!
I am the water vapor that originates from the sea,
And the water going back to the sea I am;
I am the thought and beauty of the real!
I am the attributes of the real!
I am the command of the real!
I am the one whom God has made,
The carrier of the preserved tablets;
I am the one to whom God reads out,

From these preserved tablets;

I am the one whom God has honored to be,

In His constant presence through the Perennial prayer;

I am not hypocrisy!

I am not infidelity!

I am the believer in one-Reality!

MyKoul! You are a son of man, and you are,

He who received the life from God!

59 I Promise to Keep on My Battle

I promise to keep on my battle with the evil nafs!
Until my nafs is contented and its pain recedes;
Until the Nafs e Amarah sets me free,
That has rendered me lifeless in its cage;
I promise to keep on my battle with the evil nafs!
Until the dark thoughts stop obsessing me;
Until I come close to the reality,
And delusion leaves me;
I promise to keep on my battle with the evil nafs!
Until I no longer hang on to the theory of duality;
Until the devil-nafs inside screams,
And submits to me;
I promise to keep on my battle with the evil nafs!
Until I am released from the mist of darkness,
That envelops me;
Until the real showers light upon light on me;
I promise to keep on my battle with the evil nafs!
Until my ears open and listen,
To the divine voice with clarity;
Until I do not hear anything but,
The throbbing of my heart,
Saying Allah hu; Allah hu;
I promise to keep on my battle with the evil nafs!
Until I recall my ancient covenant with my Lord;
Until I fulfill the same,
As I have already promised to do.

60 *I Love to Write Poems*

I love to write poems about 'the reality';
(Not an easy job to do)
I love to describe the all-encompassing reality,
That I've found after I left,
The philosophy of nothingness;
The crashing waves of ecstasy resonate,
In my verses about reality;
There is little talk of empty space and time!
There is only glorification of the manifest reality!
Any spurious mention of separation and differentiation,
I omit from my verses about reality;
I do not mention the 'seven wonders' and the 'seven valleys',
Told by some ancient sages before me;
I love to be positive and honest,
And just write what is purely the Absolute Unity;
I do not want to let you hopelessly ponder,
What my poem is all about;
I do not make speculations about what is the reality;
I write in my verses only,
What the real inspires me about His reality!

61 *Take a Break*

Take a break from,
Your mundane routine;
See Yourself!
Hear Yourself!
Speak to yourself!
Know yourself!
See your true self!
Notice your face,
In the mirror of reality!
You are a human being,
Feelings dwell in you,
Emotions run in you,
You have a story in you,
Beginning from eternity!
You were someone,
Before coming as man!
A conscious being!
Your essence remains the same!
You have not,
And will not change!
Let you regain,
Your consciousness!
Realize you are a living being!
You really will never die!
In your heart read the lines:
I was! I am! I will be!

It is not a crazy murmur!

It is the Real,

Speaking through you!

And with this realization,

The hotch-potch of ideas,

In your brain will evaporate!

That you are separate,

And different from the reality!

Be Quiet!

Discussions and arguments,

Do not avail here;

Pass beyond polemics;

You will then comprehend,

His reality and attributes.

62 *On the Face of Man*

On the face of Man,
God has written Bismillah;
See me in this mirror,
O you who have eyes;
Because I have made him
In my image,
To be the noblest of all creatures;
Man! Fulfill your covenant,
With your lord on the Day of Alast;
And try to prove yourself,
As His true vice-regent;
So that the angels today also,
Fall in prostration before you;
Break yourself out,
Of the cage of mud and water;
Know in yourself,
The presence of the Real;
Who brought you by His command,
From non-existence to existence;
I swear on the honor of the Real,
Who gave to Man,
Of His wisdom and knowledge,
Before He manifested Himself,
In the things of the world and humans;
Even then—Allah—existed,
As the only reality;

Think not like a blockhead,
That this beautiful manifestation,
Just happened without any command.

63 *The Real Is Manifest*

The Real is manifest in the population of the world,
And everything of the multiverse as well;
There is no room
For differentiation between one thing and the other;
Why see with the eyes that suffer from diplopic vision?
Use the eyes that have the quality of Unitary Vision!
O dervish!
Do not get involved in the exercises of meditation!
Know thou the core of remembrance and reflection!
Purify your heart from the dust of duality and differentiation!
Such that your heart becomes a clear mirror;
And when the sun shines on the mirror,
Man exclaims and says: 'I am the sun! '
The man is the mirror of the divine beauty
What shows in him is the reflection of divine attributes.

64 The Sun Coming Up Showers Clear Light

The sun coming up showers clear light;
The sleeping birds come out of their nests;
They twitter sweet songs in bushes and groves;
They are free from the state of intoxication;
Being sober is the real living, they realize;
Listen to the music of the stringless lute;
Stand up! Get out of the slumber deep!
Watch over this echoing melody sweet!
You will come closer to the reality;
The music streams flow over you;
You are totally immersed in the music divine;
The causeless music is echoing all around!
From within and from without! From right and from left!
From front and from back! From above and from below!
Do not ask me where from that music is coming;
You are yourself the real lute!
You are yourself the player of your lute!
You need not seek and search,
The source of this music out of you.

65 I Say

I say
Who thinks what I think
You say I
I say
Who sees what I see
You say I
I say
Who hears what I hear
You say I
I say
Who contemplates what I contemplate
You say I
I say
Who desires what I desire
You say I
I say
Who loves what I love
You say I
I say
Who circumambulates what I circumambulate
You say I
I say
Who is hidden and who is manifest
You say I
I say
Who is lover and who is beloved

You say I

I say

Who is seeker and who is sought

You say I

I say

Who is Zakir and who is mazkoor

You say I

I say

Who is in Anfas and who is in Afaq

You say I

I say

Who is in the heavens and who is on the earth

You say I

I say

Who are you and who am I

You say I

I say

What for my Eyes?

You say

Keep them open.

I say

What for my Ears?

You say

Keep them open.

I say

What for my Heart?

You say

What is there?

I say

Much love for you there
You say
I am much beyond your love
Keep it empty for my Secrets
I send my secrets to you,
Through your ears.
Don't plug your ears
I say
Don't hide your face
You say
Look through my veils
I say
Don't let me be without your music
You say
Get on drinking my music wine.
I say
Don't let me breathe without being with you
You say
You remember me I'll remember you.

66 *God Knows the Best*

God knows the best;

I know only what He lets me know;

What keeps me astonishing is that,

Whatever my real eyes reach,

(A flower, a thorn, a speck of grass, or a stem of chinar tree)

It turns into a lute,

And gives out melodious tunes;

I do some contemplation, and find it says:

La ilaha illa hu!

Hu! Hu! Hu! Hu!

There exists none but the one real!

I say one must constantly hear,

This holy Kalima of the Real;

Then, inshallah, he may find,

What wonderful things happen.

67 *If One Gains Sanity*

If one gains sanity, sagacity, and awareness,
He could see a hundred visions of the real being,
In the beautiful manifestation;
There are no penetrating eyes than a sage's eyes,
That could see into the core of the things;
The vision of sages discerns that the essence of all things,
In the world of creation is absolutely the One real being
Thus, they rid themselves of the delusion of duality;
Their heart is empty of the illusory differentiation!
Only the real being, they perceive,
In the beautiful creation!

68 *Those on the Way of Love*

Those on the way of love walk under cover,
So that the hosts of Satan do not hijack them;
A person of divine vision but
Recognizes the travelers on the road of love,
By their marks on their foreheads and,
Halo around their faces;
And by the words of truth and the divine knowledge,
That sprout from their mouth;
And then start following them on the road of love;
Be like such pure travelers as never leave,
Traveling to their Friend.

69 *Who Says the Eternal Being Is Not Real?*

Who says the eternal being is not real?
Who says the sun shines of its own?
One who is blindfolded, says:
I don't see anything! Nothing exists!
When you feel your eyes becoming infinite,
And perceive the infiniteness of time and space,
The eternal real you will observe in the manifestation.

70 *You Speak and I Start Listening with Care*

You speak and I start listening with care;
Your speech brings to life the dead Corpses;
I'm trying not to think of gibberish things,
When listening to your speech;
Though I was totally lost and wandering,
You brought me out of wilderness;
No one ever stays depressed and dejected,
When listening to your speech?
Those listening to your speech receive light,
And give out light;
Secrets cannot be kept hidden from a confidante!

71 *Where is the Traveler?*

Where is the traveler,
Who can travel on the road of love?
Where is the eye that can see the real in the manifestation?
Show me a man who is willing like Abraham,
To be thrown in the blazing fire
Show me a man who is willing like Moses,
To walk through Zulmaat,
For finding the water of life;
The moment this love comes to bloom in you,
You will become worthy to travel on the road of love.

72 *Man, You're So Finite*

Man, you're so finite!
How can you see the infinite being?
How can the infinite love be inside you?
Unless you understand,
How the infinite being encompasses you;
Look at the pupil in your eyes, how minute it is!
But through this small camera,
You see enormous things.

73 A Voice from Inside Sings Out

A voice from inside sings out;

At times a calm melodious voice pacifies us;

Other times excited tunes make us jubilant;

The fragrant voice spreads its fresh smell;

Get up and take that voice in;

It is this sweet voice,

That lets lovers live;

Breathe, before you're gone with the wind!

74 *Night Comes So People Can Take Rest*

Night comes so people can take rest,
Like birds in their cozy nests;
Then day follows the night;
Some people get up for their business;
Others go to their schools:
To learn,
Knowledge and wisdom from their teachers;
Learning and teaching are the prime activities of life!

75 *Swallows Go Back*

Swallows go back,
To where they come from;
Everyone returns home one day;
Swallows, when you get there,
Do not forget me please;
I love you! I will wait for you!

76 *Listen to the Voices*

Listen to the voices inside my poems;
Let them guide you to where they will;
Follow those clear hints to know the secrets;
And never turn a deaf ear to words of wisdom.

77 *At First, I Listened to Songs*

At first, I listened to songs and concerts;
Losing my precious time of remaining awake,
For night prayers, zikr, and meditation;
Now, more intense, calm and composed, I am
When rain falls, fire flames douse!

78 *What Is Being and What Is Non-Being?*

What is Being and what is non-being?

I do not know?

In my view, only Being exists;

Non-Being does not, and can never be;

The reality is not what it seems to be.

Being is one, unique, unborn, and indestructible;

SAY: 'He - Allah - is the One:

Allah the Eternal, the Uncaused Cause of All Being!

He begets not, and neither is He begotten;

And there is nothing that could be compared with Him!

79 *No Intellect Denies*

No intellect denies that you are the reality;
Only a few know that you are their reality;
Very few give in completely to the reality,
That there is no place where you are not;
Yet you are not seen by any human eye;
But yes, you can be seen in the mirrors,
Of the manifestation.

80 *From the Real Source*

From the real source comes,
The sound of a flute;
The flute is not made of the reed;
The flutist is himself,
The listener of his own flute;
He sips the flute-music like wine;
He flutes more and more,
And sips the music more;
Until he is fully drunk;
He starts to fall into the high clear silence,
And forgets all images and impressions of duality.

81 *One Day I Might Be*

One day I might be,
Completely out of the delusion of duality,
I will know the reality that,
The angels could not know.
The real will write on my tablets,
The poems about my reality,
That I haven't so far thought of!

82 *You Are What You Are!*

You are what You are!

I am what I am!

Your love in my heart!

My heart not the organ of body!

With music resonating inside!

I have no name for,

What resonates so perfectly!

Giving me peace and tranquility!

I remember You! You remember Me!

I love You! You love Me!

I am Your bd! You are my Maula!

I am not You! You are not Me!

Of Your spirit You have blown into me!

Who is then my essence other than you!

83 *Listen, If You Can!*

Listen, if you can!
Listening means connecting to the Friend;
Listening means listening to silence;
Listening transports you to a place,
Where the ear sits inside the eyes.

84 *You Come to Reading the Book of Life*

You come to reading the book of life;
If you see the book is sealed:
Don't hurry! Don't worry!
Do not be tired and ready to quit;
Let your ears hear the divine music;
Let your eyes see the divine light;
Let your real intellect shine,
With the divine intellect;
The seal of the book will break forthwith;
And you will read into the codes,
The real meaning of life!

85 *Keep Walking on the Path of Love*

Keep walking on the path of love,
Though there's no place to get to;
Don't try to see through the distances because,
That's not for lovers true;
Move within, to see your reality;
But don't move the way quest to see,
Someone other makes you move.

86 *Remembering Allah Heals Me*

Remembering Allah heals me;

Not remembering Him,

I feel the doors closing on me;

I would not wish for anyone else the absence,

From eternal remembrance;

Verily, in the remembrance of Allah,

Do hearts find rest!

87 *I Pretended to Fix My Gaze*

I pretended to fix my gaze,
To see if I could see the real;
One day I realized the reality,
That the Real is actually here,
I have not to arrive anywhere,
Nothing of reality is distant,
The real is present everywhere,
Nothing is left to arrive.

88 *Here is a Magnificent Preacher*

Here's a magnificent preacher
Holding out Fat books,
Reading out long passages,
To me, I hope, not for me!

89 The Prophets, Sages, Mystics, and Divine Philosophers

The prophets, sages, mystics, and divine philosophers,
Tell and share with us precious secrets,
That descends on them from the Universal Intellect;
They all are born of a woman,
They aren't supernatural beings;
But still the great sign of the truth and reality,
A guidance to people to know the reality!

90 The Real Lover Is Graceful

The real lover is graceful, rational, and realistic;
Someone sober, not lost in delusion,
He doesn't ever worry or fear about the love affair;
He annihilates from his mind all inclinations,
Except his love for the real.

91 *The Food of Spirituality*

The food of spirituality cannot be eaten,
Nor the pearls of wisdom can we get from barren minds,
Nor the knowledge can we get,
By looking at the face of our teacher,
There is a secret core in everything of manifestation,
Not even Gabriel can know without the divine intelligence.

92 *I Pretended to Fix My Gaze*

I pretended to fix my gaze,
To see if I could see the real;
One day I realized the reality,
That the Real is actually here;
I have not to arrive anywhere;
Nothing of reality is hidden;
The real is present everywhere;
Nothing is left to arrive!

93 *There Is No Religion but Love*

There is no religion but love;
No scriptures, no rituals, yet a pure religion;
The Friend calls from there:
Why do you hesitate when the road is clear!

94 *Knowledge and Wisdom Are Gifts from the Real*

Knowledge and wisdom are gifts from the Real;
In the frame of skin and veins,
The teacher -Divine Intellect - abides within,
Know this Sheikh and become a student,
To know the Truth and the Reality!

95 *Out of His Command*

Out of His Command, 'Be!',
The Real manifests His reality,
Through humans and non-humans in the multiverse,
Where the real exhibits his own beauty to Himself;
Nothing exists here except by His command 'Be!'
Read His command 'Be! And it is!',
Mentioned in the Book of His creation!

96 *Divine Intellect Is Like a Sieve*

Divine intellect is like a sieve to filter the nafs,
It reveals impurities of nafs and removes duality,
It shows the light of the Real who throws,
His radiance into the man and the universe.

97 *The One Who Floods My Heart*

The one who floods my heart and mind with His zikr,
Who takes away from me the thoughts of duality,
Who drags and throws me in His sanctuary,
That Unitary Divine Presence,
Is the source of poems I write.

98 The Illusion Clears

The illusion clears,

Knowing comes;

The reality is not like a dead corpse;

But the reality is hidden from eyes;

As a diamond is hidden in the stone!

99 *Your Reality Does Not Begin*

Your reality does not begin,
When you're conceived,
It is the eternal light that is your essence,
Your reality cannot hide in the envelope of your body,
It gives off radiance that illuminates your intellect.

100 All Day and Night

All day and night, the eternal zikr,
A wordless, quiet, soundless zikr,
Reed song, a secret between you and the Real,
If this song stops, the light goes off.

101 *Sleep and Slumber the Real Has Not*

Sleep and slumber the Real has not,
Night and day the Real is watching you,
Stop looking for the Real,
When you're sleeping,
Wake up - He is before you,
You will see the Real,
At dusk and dawn!

102 *The Life Extends into Eternity*

The life extends into eternity,
Truly knowing this is what awareness is,
Not knowing it is ignorance about reality,
And it is the lack of enlightenment.

103 *The World of Manifestation*

The world of manifestation,
Is not as we on its face see;
But if we go into its different things,
We may appreciate its divine beauty;
And may find insight into the One reality.
The colors and the patterns of the world,
When we see with the divine eye,
Tell us about the inherent reality,
That we normally might not see;
Lord, give us all knowledge and wisdom,
To set us free from the illusion of mind.
How will we see the manifestation,
Separate and different from the reality,
When we see that in all ways,
All things are of the same reality;
All manifestation is in essence,
The expression of the same reality!
So much of differentiation we may take,
For granted to exist in the manifestation;
But our perception about reality can change,
When we have a transparent glass view,
Of the world of manifestation;
There is no manifestation except the single reality!

104 *Ever Since My First Birth*

Ever since my First birth I've loved You;
Neither I knew your face nor your name;
A voice from my within and out of me,
Constantly hearing I have been;
Telling me that Me and the whole creation,
Is in essence one and the same;
The reality is like a shapeless flame,
Facing all the directions!
A formless reality in exquisite manifestation!
Worshipped that all-in-all reality must be!
Far, far beyond human comprehension!
When, where, and how it came to be!
Except the lovely glorious manifestation nothing one can see!
My soul opens its eyes to love the sight,
And opens its ears to hear the melodious music;
How else could I vision the beauty of the beautiful?
Love cannot be there unless,
The subtle reality takes the body of manifestation;
As such what the real is, and who,
I bid my love to see in the beauty;
Now that the real has come out in its manifestation,
I fix my unwavering gaze at it,
And bow to the beauty expressed in the manifestation;
Nothing veils the reality from my sight!
It scatters its light bright through the manifestation!

105 *Having Passed Away*

Having passed away from self-alienation from the Real,
I realized it was my ignorance, and delusion,
That all along I had considered my self-having,
A separate identity, existing of its own,
Apart from the real which is an Absolute Unity;
The illusion of my separation from the real blazed into flames!
A path to Thy reality, thus, by your guidance, did I find!
But Lord! No creature like Iblis—who has avowed to lead me astray,
May draw me away from the religion of your reality;
I can no longer live, my Lord, without the belief,
That you are my reality;
Your reality is everywhere: how can I flee from the truth?
I have desired through hope to acquire from Thee,
Knowledge about your Absolute unity;
You have opened in me the eye of divine intellect!
I very clearly see the beautiful design of your reality!
Lo! I have severed every thought of alienation and separation from me;
My imagined separate selfhood has died!
Now, no one can banish from my heart the light of your absolute unity!

106 *Look into the Morning Sun*

Look into the morning sun
Melting the pearls of dew drops
Dew goes back to the sea
Reflect, your journey is circular
No beginning, no ending
This is the reality of the Real.

107 *Reconciliation*

Strangers pass around me;
They who are my brothers, neighbors, relatives;
I have no obligation towards the person,
Who stops,
And tells me: 'I know you,'
I tried to look into his eyes,
To see my pic;
And not finding me there,
I took my way back,
And walked through the crowd,
Without looking back;
When he realizes,
His ungratefulness, and his betrayal,
He will return to where I wait;
When he sees me,
He will give me a big hug;
Tears will roll down my eyes,
And I'll forgive him;
Who will I be?
Who will he be?
We'll not exchange regrets!

108 *Look at the Mirror of Heart*

If you wish to know the reality of self,
Look at the mirror of your heart;
When the sun of reality shines,
It radiates light and brightness;
When the night of silence falls,
There resonates deep, sweet music;
Just as the ripples and waves,
Create music in the still ocean!

109 *Golden Beacon*

To know The Real
Cleanse your mind of illusion
Knowledge comes with awareness,
The Way is neither long nor crooked;
A middle way - that is straight and shortest;
A calm and quiet traveler treads this.
The resolute traveler, with the staff of Moses;
Nothing more needed, only Divine intellect!
Climbing the mount Tour,
When the enlightenment arrives
Shut your mouth,
Don't talk too much about it,
To every Tom, Dick, and Harry;
Just live it in your own way,
The travelers in the dark alleys,
Need the divine light,
That sharpens their intellect,
To know the deep meaning,
That Light comes naturally
Blessing and mercy of God,
The fragrance of blossoms calls the bees;
They come in a twinkling of an eye for the nectar
Our time in this world is so short,
To avoid regret, let us behave as bees
And not miss the opportunity to collect,
The nectar of immortality,

Like a torchbearer showing light,
To travelers on a moonless night,
Divine intellect guides our passage,
Through this transitory world;
In the short sojourn here in this world,
Of darkness and pain,
Let us keep on lighting,
The golden beacon of love and peace!

If we give up trying to search it outside;
Outside ourselves or outside His manifestation
We are never cut off from reality!
The search for reality is the quest,
To gain knowledge of the divine Self;
To regain the Edenic peace;
To become a faithful servant of God;
To get the Promised station in his presence;
To meet sages and be their companions;
To benefit from their knowledge and wisdom; and
To live in harmony in the world of manifestation.
We are all pilgrims in this world, seeking
To see the earthly paradise,
That God had created before sending us here;
The task we are given is to realize our reality,
And see the presence of the real in his manifestation.
But like a spider, we have woven a web of,
Superstitions, mythic beliefs, and illusions:
We continue to build icons and create gods;
We worship their images, graves, mausoleums;
We create and follow religions that are bent outwards;
We reject the teaching that could turn us inwards;
We're an outward-looking people;
We have become extroverts in our actions;
We're inclined to what is unreal and misleading;
We're sanctimonious in our disposition;

We are away from reality,

We have no sincerity.

111 A Feeling of Hope

A feeling of hope when you wake up,
Is a sure sign that you put your faith in the Real!
Your desire to see into the essence of everything,
Is a sure sign that Allah wants you to see his reality,
In the world of His manifestation;
He is not a hidden secret,
If you have the real eyes to see;
Your aspiration which asks you to discern the reality,
Can only help you break through the walls surrounding the reality;
Give yourself a rest from searching the reality!
When the Real is revealing Himself to Himself!
When will you start realizing,
That He is your reality?

112 The Spring Rain is Falling

The spring rain is falling,
Constantly for two days,
Creating a soft music sound;
Rain whispers to me,
Hear the celestial music!
Rain musician beating drumsticks,
On the rooftops, hilltops, and human tops,
Creating the mellow music all around;
Bidding to recollect the ancient music!
Chords of my heart are awakened;
Notes of melodious music,
Rise and fall over my eyes and ears;
I am forbidden to expose the secret,
Hidden in the rise and fall of music!
Soft, gentle, and mellow music,
Produced with rain sticks,
Remind me of the music of heaven;
God, the Great Musician,
Calling: bring your ears near to Me,
And hear the immortal sound!

113 *The Whole World is Bleeding*

The whole world is bleeding,
A nation is coming over another nation
The ferocious wild beasts are ruling
The lambs and kids are shivering
The Falcon brings the message to the suffering
The father says I am sending my hordes
To free the people and give them peace
Over the whole earth they are coming.
The Cow is giving the message to people,
In my name, you will be killed and lynched
But I will never deny my streams of milk,
To you or to your children
Krishna will again walk in the land with flocks of cows
To offer milk to all people free of cost
My children, my children, wake up! wake up!
Look up to see the morning star on your head,
It is telling you to rise up, the brilliant sun is rising,
Wear the light of the sun on your soul and body!
I show the light to you, my children,
I show the light to you, my children,
Come out of darkness! Come out of darkness!

114 *For Me: World is Not All Empty*

For me: world is not all empty;
It is the precious treasure of the Real!
Death and Life, Day and Night,
Go after each other,
As the seasons of the year go;
The heart of man, after transformation,
Knows, and sees the reality.
The Truth from inside cries out:
I am much closer to you,
Than the distance between Two Bows;
I am the Real! You are my manifestation!

115 *Satan's Voice Sleeps There*

Satan's voice sleeps there,
Where the soul dives into the musical stream;
The touch of music awakens the soul,
And carries it on its untouchable wings,
To where celestial bells are clearly heard;
The soul for the first time listens,
The verses from the Archangel Gabriel,
From the book of knowledge,
Inscribed on the Preserved Tablets.
Shaken, never had heard the verses before!
The Prophet comes down from the cave!
Khadija opens the door of home!
Finds her beloved transformed into a new person!
Recites the first verses of the Qur'an,
To the people of Home;
They hear and believe!
Those who knew him never questioned him!
How could they?
They heard the message in joy,
And sincerely acted upon it till their life.
And the Satan was dead and life smiled again!
The seekers of truth, one by one, came to him, and said:
Speak to us of the Divine message,
Revealed for our guidance through you;
And he raises his head and reads out to them:

READ in the name of thy Sustainer, who has created,
Created man out of a germ-cell!
Read - for thy Sustainer is the Most Bountiful One!
Who has taught [man] the use of the pen!
Taught man what he did not know!
The people heard with awe,
And there fell a magical stillness upon them;
And in a sweet voice he spoke to them:
When the Qur'an is read,
Listen to it with attention,
And hold your peace:
That ye may receive Mercy.
What Qur'an beckons to you, follow it,
Though the commands might be hard for you,
And might shatter your Worldly dreams,
Because when you accept the commands,
The angels of God will unfold their wings for you!

116 *Even if You Consume*

Even if you consume whole of your lifetime,
Listening to Chakri and Qawwali,
At the banks of the Lidder river or in seclusion at your home,
It is not as good as really catching flies in the air;
One word of wisdom:
If you want to know the prime secret,
Here it is: the Real can be found in the Heart,
And in the beautiful manifestation out of the Heart.

117 *The flowering season has died*

The flowering season has died;
The colorful flowers go on falling;
The nightingale is calling;
Silence penetrates its song;
The Wordless!
The Voiceless!
The Equanimity!
The reality of the Real!
Preparing to bloom in the Spring;
Preparing to visit the rose garden;
To enjoy the beauty and fragrance,
Of colorful roses;
And sing the song of ecstasy!
Giving thanks to Himself,
For manifesting His power!

118 *Alone, I Watch the Rain*

Alone, I watch the rain,
Washing the mountains,
Flowing down in rivers,
Walking back to the seas.

119 Past is Dead

Past is dead;
The dead do not arise!
Present breathing;
Until the last breath it exhales;
Future uncertain!
Future unpredictable!
Future unattainable!
Yet for the people of vision,
As clear as the moon,
In the cloudless sky!
In the last watch of night,
The cool Breeze blows gently;
The moonlit window smells of roses;
Wake up! From sleep!
The sun is rising!
The new day is breaking!
The day and the night alternate!
Life moves on its circular path!

Yes! My Lord, on this Night of Power,
The night better than a thousand nights!
When You sent down the Holy Quran,
For the eternal guidance of humankind,
On the Heart of your chosen one, Muhammad!
Your Honor, grant us what we ask Tonight:
All your blessings - Earthly and The Divine!
Do not withdraw from us your profound love!
Grant all things that make us your perfect servants!
Release us from the trap of our evil nafs!
And let our nafs be contented,
With the manifestation of your reality;
That you have hidden in us on the day of our creation;
When of your spirit you have blown into us;
Amen! Amen! Amen!

121 *The Load on My Brain*

The load on my brain I set aside;
Thus little disturbance remains there;
In silence and perfect composure I meditate,
On the cherishing melodious tunes,
Coming constantly from heaven;
I don't have to bother to strum over the strings of any lute;
There's a divine breeze sweeping over the strings;
And the divine lute plays itself without my effort.

Alif Lam Mim,

The great book isn't difficult,

For those who are righteous and ward off evil;

Let go of following the Satan of nafs, your evil ego;

And the book of knowledge will be perfectly clear;

When you cling to a hairbreadth of distinction,

You will not vision the absolute unity;

If you want to realize the truth,

Bear in mind what is told by the Truth:

'We will show them Our Signs in the universe,

And in their own selves,

Until it becomes manifest to them that this is the truth';

The struggle between good and evil must go on within your selves,

Until the disease of the mind is cured well,

And goodness wins the fight;

Your effort in this regard is just grasping,

The deeper meaning of truth;

The evil will then stop itself troubling the peace of your mind;

Your reality is as vast as the infinite space and time!

It is perfect and lacks nothing, you must believe in it;

Because you select your external nature,

And reject the inner truth,

You can't perceive your true nature,

On which you really are born;

Don't get entangled in the ephemeral worldly things;

Don't lose yourself in the wilderness of emptiness;

Be at peace in the oneness of reality, and,
All confusion of duality will disappear;
Asserting that the world of manifestation is real,
You become a seer of the deeper reality;
Denying that the world of manifestation is real,
You become blind to the one reality of all the things;
The more you think about the differences and distinctions,
The farther you are from the truth of oneness;
Step aside from all thinking of plurality,
You will find yourself the way to unity;
Returning to the root, you find the real meaning;
Go into appearances, you will get to their source;
At the moment you gain insight of the divine intellect,
You transcend the outer appearance of the manifestation;
Don't keep searching for the truth here and there,
The truth is nearer to you than your jugular vein;
Just let go of your deception and delusion!
For the heart in harmony with the reality,
All duality and illusion disappear;
With even a trace of doubt about the book of guidance,
You can never know the meaning of the verses of wisdom;
All at once you are free from ignorance about the reality!
With no trace of unreal images left on your mind!
All manifestation is real, true, and perfect,
In its being the manifestation of the powers of the Real!
In the world of manifestation, when you see its essence,
You will at once say
'Nothing exists except the real!'

123 *I Have Come Here*

I have come here from a place without limits,
Inhabited by the eternal Truth;
I am striving to come out of the wilderness and,
Go back to inhabit in that eternal abode;
Sometimes I climb the peak of Illiyeen;
Sometimes I play in the down world of Saafileen;
But most of the time I relax in peace,
And speak of neither profit nor loss;
Even if the world became a grove of gold trees,
It wouldn't mean a fig for me;
Cause who can live on gold?

124 *Snow on Mountain Peaks*

Snow on mountain peaks
Gushing water in mountain streams
All flowing downwards back to the seas
The beautiful landscape
As we know
Belongs to those who have aesthetic sense,
To appreciate the beauty of manifestation
The upper worlds inhabited by light spirits
The lower worlds inhabited by fire spirits
Originally are one - they're of the same reality
There is not a bit of dust on the mirror of seers
They have got only full, perfect, and clear,
Enlightenment and awareness.

125 Kneel to True Teachers

Kneel to true teachers and listen,
To their wise words as a devout student.
The best comprehension is the way of 'non-comprehension',
The radiance of the Divine intellect!
The best treasure is what cannot be looked for,
The priceless treasure of the Real itself.
The most bitter truth is 'transcendent reality'.
That reality, though difficult to know, is the real reality!
The life-giving drink is 'not drinking the cup of death',
Taking the nectar of immortality!
It is the drink of 'I am reality'!
Oh, this realization needs no spiritual guru,
Awareness is a gift of Divine intellect!
This enlightenment is beyond words and description!
The divine intellect is not the lesson of children,
Nor is it,
When you reach the truth of 'non-comprehension',
You receive the highest knowledge divine.
When you perceive the real in his beautiful manifestation,
You realize the sublime truth!
If you approach the truth of 'reality' through Divine intellect,
You follow the supreme path.
When you know that you are the viceregent of the Real,
The ultimate knowledge you've obtained!
When you see the futility of reason, that is the supreme logic.
When you know that high and low realms are of the same Real

You have entered the real city of knowledge!
Discriminating between good and evil,
Opens the way to perfect wisdom.
Experiencing the dissolution of duality,
You will come to realize the existence of a single reality!
Observing the truth of 'manifestation',
Opens the way to see absolute unity.
Going beyond 'it is?' and 'it is not',
Opens the way to perfect belief!
When you realize the truth of 'Deen',
You have reached the highest purpose in life.
Ignorant are those who lack this truth!
Do not choose as your guides on your spiritual journey,
Fake teachers inflated by learning books of others,
Scholars bragging about their empty words,
And Sufis seduced by illusory images,
Give your ear to this warning of Rumi – the great master of the path!
For though they pose to be Gnostics and friends of God,
They want to enslave you and catch you in their net,
The way a hunter catches the innocent birds.

126 *There Isn't Any Mystery*

Actually, there isn't any mystery;
Much more than dust to be wiped away;
He who wants to know the reality;
Need not sit stiff in Yoga posture;
Sitting like a motionless statue in the temple;
Renouncing the beautiful World of the Real;
Poor unreal seeker of the Real!
Ever immersed in illusory scenes!
Open the eyes and ears of your divine intellect;
Until a flash of lightning shows,
Hidden and manifest are dust on mirror.

127 *The Real is Something No Eyes Can See*

The Real is something that no eyes can see
Save knowing it's there, there's nothing to know
The comprehensions of created natures cannot get to reality
The perception of reality is difficult to acquire
Much more difficult is the perception of the reality of the Reality
The Real is beyond what we assume to be the Real
No human vision can encompass Him
Whereas He encompasses all human vision
For He alone is unfathomable, all-aware
The sun shines bright above our heads
But who can look at the sun
Without losing the sight?
Who can see the Real
Besides seeing His manifestation?
If you want to see the Real, look at His manifestation
That blooms like divine roses all around

128 *Neither Seeking Fame*

Neither seeking fame
Nor grieving my seclusion
I hide deep in the silence
Far from worldly furor
Years of life ending
Weaving poems on mystic themes
Withdrawing from public chatting
Who will befriend me?
Wisdom inscribed on hidden scrolls
Seekers sleeping, wrapped in darkness
Even in the last watch of the night
My poems might remain unread

129 *The Abiding-place of the Real*

The abiding-place of the Real
Has no boundaries
East, west, north or south
You are the lote tree in the middle of it
Turning your head
You can look to each direction
And for the first time find
That your eyes have been deceiving you
As a matter of fact, the Real
Is in each direction
And to Allah—the Real—belong east, west, north and south
And wherever you turn to
There is His countenance
Behold, the Real is infinite, and all-knowing

130 *The Great City of Knowledge Has No Gate*

The Great City of knowledge has no gate
This is an unwalled city
The thousand roads enter it
There are no check-posts on the roads
All seekers have a free entry to this city
When one gets into this unwalled city
He freely obtains awareness and enlightenment
This great city is within you
Long seeking to go into this city
I tried first to go with others to this city
I was far from reaching it
Now I walk all alone to this city
I meet it everywhere
It is just I myself
And I am now within myself
Understanding this way
I found I am the real city of knowledge

131 *Walking Through the Zulmat*

Walking through the Zulmat
Not having found the lifewater, like Moses
Walking back I found to my surprise
The spring of liwater.er is within my home
Singing with ecstasy
I am taking cup after cup
Happily passing the day
Flitting here and there
Swinging my head
I impress my own self
That I've found the spring of life-water

132 *The Chinar Tree Sways in Joy*

The chinar tree sways in joy
Sweet sound streams up and up
There's eternal word in sound
My heart loses itself to the sound
The waves of the sound strike
Against the walls of my soul
A cool touch wakes up my memory
Of the sweet music in paradise
Warms up my urge to go back home
I'll wait calmly on the gate of paradise
Until Rizwan allows me inside
And horis start to sing welcome songs
Time is singing on the divine song
Of 'I am the truth! I am the real!'
Somehow, here and now, I am hearing.

133 My Heart and My Nafs Have Both Settled Down

My heart and my nafs have both settled down
Into perfect peace and tranquility
Light upon light shines bright my divine intellect
That makes me feel the presence of the Real
Under and above the surface of the creation
The enormous face of my familiar Real I see
As one sees the face of the moon at night in a clear pond
Though I know it is ever impossible to see the source of this reflection
When I see the reflection
All my shrillness fades into the sound of silence
But, now and then, thick clouds float over the pond
It confuses me a lot, at that moment
As I'm unable to see the reflection
But not enough to make me forget
The presence of the moon in the sky

134 *Striving to Broom Away the Evil Thoughts*

Striving to broom away the evil thoughts
You become part of what's evil
Strive to cultivate the good thoughts
The evil thoughts will get weeded out
Ceasing contemplating on images is
In fact the real contemplation
So how do you gain control and get beyond the unreal?
Open those eyes—the ones that are in your spirit!

135 No Need to Glide and Fly Like Birds in the Air

No need to glide and fly like birds in the air
The same Real is in the heavens
And the same Real is on the ground
No wisdom in asking for the miracles
When you're yourself the chief miracle of the Real
No point swimming back to the origin
When the river is flowing around you in all directions
Is it not absurd to count the ripples in the ocean?
When you're yourself the real ocean
No point travelling in search of the Real
When the Real is not apart from you
The invisible Real and the manifestation of the Real
Where is there any difference?

136 *Born by the Will of Allah at the Beginning*

Born by the will of Allah at the beginning
Of the manifestation by the command 'Be'
All other beings of intellect—the angels and the jinni
Were turned upside down
I am Adam and so have an intense urge in my heart
To climb straight on to the lofty summits
To view the beautiful manifestation of the Real
Between my eyes a divine eye sees the Beautiful World
In beautiful colors and shapes
I find the Real in pure beauties that He created
To adorn the empty-multiverse
The real in me holds up the eyes to look up
To see His light in all His manifestation
As I dive in the 'Ocean of my Knowing-intellect
The Pearls of wisdom shine forth by themselves
Space brightened by the light of the Real, I see it telling:
I am the independent!
I am the Real! I am the truth!
So I throw my net and catch the dragon of my nafs
To burn it to ashes
It is the barrier between me and the Real
Alone I walk with a view to
Connecting to the Real through its manifestations!

137 *This is an Exquisite Truth*

This is an exquisite truth:
Sages aren't just the ordinary folks
They aren't of the same intellect
Speculating about no basic difference
Is like equating a chimpanzee and a humane
When you've a strong philosophical intellect
You can then alone know the divine reality
Once you know the Reality
Intuition and cognitive power will intensify
You'll become familiar with your essence
Your illusions about the Real
Will give way to the awareness
Your heart-well will sprout
The springs of divine knowledge and wisdom

138 *And My Spirit is Longing*

And my spirit is longing
To fly to the highest heaven
Its desire to know the Real
Moves the Real
To lend grace to my spirit
And vision to know the Real
Within! And everywhere!
The Kingdom of the Real! It's just before my vision!
Just behind the veils
But the transparent veils! For the persons of vision!
Law of the Real is without error
The sovereign of the Kingdom is the Real
The clauses, sections, and the subsections
Of the Law of the Real are real
And this Law reveals to the seers
The omnipotence of the Real

139 *You Are the Beginning of the Book of Reality*

You are the beginning of the book of reality!
You are the start of the verses of the Real!
You are the glorification of His manifestation!
You are the start of recitation by the Real!
You are the verses of His song of Love!
Love that made Him to come out of darkness!
Love that daily is expressed by the Real!
As He manifests and re-manifests His reality!
He is sitting on His throne of glory with His book
Rejoice! Rejoice! You subject of His poems!
See the Real king on the throne of glory!
Writing and reciting His poems about His glory!
See the beauty of the real in you and around!
And dance in joy around the throne of His glory!
See, you are created in the image of the Real!
You are the chief manifestation of the Real!
Exult, exult, O precious manifestation of the Real!
So marvelously fashioned! In the best proportion!
Be glad! He is casting the light of reality upon you!
As a bride is gladdened in her bridal-chamber!

140 My Lord, Your Reality is Not Shrouded in Mystery

O My Lord, Your reality is not shrouded in mystery
Your Presence is manifest, not hidden in mystery
You made my heart as the Temple for my worship
I hear Your praise in delightful tunes in this temple
I offer the perpetual prayer with devotion in this temple
My prayers bring to my vision great pillars of light
I get fathomless delight in the recitation of Your Quran
You reveal to me the secrets of your book verse by verse
Then I wake up, and I see You are the real, O Lord
And I give thanks to You for it is pleasant to give thanks!
On knowing my reality, my origin, my truth
I proclaim: one who knows his reality has known the Real!

141 *Lord, Where Shall I Find You Not?*

Lord, where shall I find You not?
The throne of Your majesty covers the heavens and the earth
Your place is lofty and secret, deep within me
Lord where shall I find You not?
The seven skies and the whole earth
And all that in and between them
Is Your glorious manifestation!
Lord where shall I find you not?
You are the innermost and the outermost reality!
You are beyond the limitations of Time and space!
Lord where shall I find you not?
Your earth and your heavens cannot encompass You!
The heart of Your believing servant but encompasses You!
Lord where shall I find you not?
You have made the Earth a vast expanse
And adorned it with all the essential things
You have erected seven high skies
Without pillars over our head
You have made the sun a brightly burning lamp
For our light and heat
Lord where shall I find you not?
You are praised by Your hosts in heavens and the earth
Even their praise is not sufficient to explain your reality!
You are the real manifested in all the things of your creation
Lord where shall I find you not?
You are praised in masjids, temples and synagogues

But no one can praise you as you praise yourself!

You are above everything

But You are nearer to the Gnostics' vision

Lord where shall I find you not

My sight, my hearing, my speech, my feeling attest

That there is no creator except You!

Lord where shall I find you not?

I seek to know You with my intellect

I constantly remember You with all my heart

When I go out towards You

I find You coming towards me

I look upon Your wondrous power and awe

Wherever I turn to

How can I say that I have not seen You?

The multiverse and their inhabitants proclaim

Your tasbih—without a sound

How can I say that I have not heard your word?

My thoughts flow from you through my brain

That issue on my tongue

And express through my actions and deeds

How can I say You are not my real?

142 A Voice Arose from the Mount Faraan

A voice arose from the mount Faraan
That the awaited messenger has come
To convey unto the people His messages
A voice to cause them to grow in purity
A voice to impart unto them the divine writ
As well as wisdom
A voice that brings to life the dead
A voice that comes forth from all the sides
A voice that glorifies the lord of the universe
The Sovereign Supreme, the Holy, the Almighty, the Wise!
A voice that echoes in deserts and dales
A voice that is like a roaring lion
A voice that reveals the secrets hidden
A voice that declares ***la illaha illallah***
A voice that proclaims ***Muhammadur-rasoolullah***
A voice that is eternal, and never expires
A voice that brings out humankind from darkness to light
A voice that blazes and sparkles the fire of love
A voice that causes peace in heart and mind
A voice that sounds without instruments
A voice that Adam first heard in the heaven
A voice to which all the angels prostrated
A voice whose waves are like flashes of light!

143 *On Coming Near to the Forbidden Tree*

On coming near to the forbidden tree
He frowns and asks me to leave the paradise
On leaving the God's sanctuary:
I listened to my guilt, and my Spirit wept
In its asking for forgiveness
I repented and supplicated to my God:
'Our Lord, we have wronged ourselves
And if You do not forgive us and have mercy upon us
We will surely be among the losers.'
Though my ego balks to accept my guilt
My heart is full with remorse, and is uneasy
So I pledge to live as the modest being
And walk as such on the earth as a pure servant
With my head raised toward the heaven
What good is the wealth and luxuries of the world
When the spirit is in pain?
The worldly thoughts are but worried about me:
For closing my eyes at the fine physiques of damsels
They mock me for my unworldly lifestyle
They look with wonder at my eyes
Swollen and reddened with night vigil
And not a one of the worldly thoughts speaks wisely
Their souls are blunted, their eyes are blurred
They are the goat-footed thinkers
How can a person of knowledge and wisdom
Hold back from longing toward rising to heights?

By God and God's beloved
I'll keep my oaths
I'll climb the cliffs; and ascend to the uppermost summit
And cast my glances at the beautiful manifestation of the Real
Until the word "God is beautiful, and He loves His beauty" makes sense to me.

144 In the Very Beginning, Before Man's Creation

In the very beginning, before man's creation
He was just a hidden treasure
He, then, brought me forth from Nothing
And endowed me with sight, hearing, and speech
With these divine powers he asked me to see and appreciate his beauty in his beautiful manifestation
But at the end of time, I shall be summoned back after resurrection
My life flowed out of the depth of his supreme spirit
After giving me form and order
He blew into me of his intellect
Divine command created me for being as his vice-regent!
And so he taught me from His book of knowledge the names of all the things
Then, he presented me before the assembly of angels
As a being full with knowledge and wisdom
They all submitted to me except Iblis, the ignorant
He didn't know of the treasure
That God had invested in me
Then, He shined his light on me
To lead me in the dark alleys of the earth
He sprouted from my within the hidden springs
On my left and on my right
He made me descend the steps

Leading down from the Paradise to the earth

To be here as his faithful servant!

145 *You Must Know It Quite Well*

You must know it quite well
That deep within you, there is only:
A single truth!
A single reality!
A single essence!
And that is called the Real!
Well, that has no particular name
Rather that has got all names
Then, if you understand this reality
Do not resist it; do not flee from it
It is your salvation!
It is your awareness!
And it is your enlightenment!

146 Make Me Like a Falcon on the Heights of Your Skies

Make me like a falcon on the heights of your skies
And set me like a watcher on your world of manifestation
Give me the wine of your love to drink
And cause me intoxication
And satisfy me with your melodious voice
On the day of my resurrection
Place the cup of marifat upon my right hand
So that my tongue of intellect gives voice to the pearls of wisdom
Make me sing in joy your praise to glorify you
In response to your eternal song of love
For countless years I have declared my faith in your absolute oneness
Sitting behind my eyes, I've been in constant prayer
I am grateful to You, my Love
For you've always answered my prayer.

147 And the Real Spoke to Me When I Saw His Name

And the Real spoke to me when I saw His name
Written on the wallpaper of my heart with the ink of His light
Illuminating my intellect with His knowledge and wisdom:
And the Real said to me:
'Behold, I am the name of the poem, that you read in the book of your heart!
Behold, I am the beauty that you see with your heart's eyes!
Behold, I am the secret word that you hear in your heart!
When your eyes and ears see and hear my name and my signs
I reveal to you the tremendous difference between you and me
But, at the same time I astonish you when secretly I whisper to you:
You are from me, I have of my spirit blown into you.'
And there raged a war in my heart between the evil and the good:
And by the grace of the Real, the light over the darkness was victorious
And the Light from the Real illuminated all days of my life
And so my nafs was contented finding the light within me
As such I offer all praises to the Real in my heart forever.

148 I Thought I Would Not Be Able to Find You Here

I thought I would not be able to find you here
I didn't recognize that you aren't a stranger to me
I didn't recognize your face in the mirrors around.
You said to me the last time:
'wherever you turn to I'm there
It's the last time
Don't roam around in wilderness anymore
Breaking every barrier, removing all the veils
See that I am my manifestation
I have not hidden my face
Behind the piles of darkness over darkness.'
Now, I find you illuminating me and all the universe
This all ends my ignorance right here
Now, I realize:
You're the reality of my life
That has never to die.
O the Living! this is me standing before You
This is me bowing my head to You in ruku
This is me prostrating to you on my forehead
Saying all the prayers that have no words and voice
This is me finding rock bottom
Realizing that there is still a road to go ahead
And that the road to the Real has got no ending
Thinking that you have fully known the Real

Is an unrealistic assumption
In truth, the inability to comprehend is the real cognition
This is me giving the further research away
He is what He is, He is the Real
Nobody can give His better definition
Than How He tells about Himself in His scripture
I know that is the only sound definition
It's the only definition I've got to comprehend
And believe with conviction.

149 *The Glaring Bright Beams*

The glaring bright beams,
sneaking through the window silts!
I gaze at them in wonder, for the lone reason
That they come from the lamp of eternity
The holy beams of light brighten the soul with ecstasy
These splendid beams are the messengers of the divine knowledge
and wisdom
Coupled with grand, sweet tunes of divine melody
They open the ears and eyes of the intellect
To join the dervish to supreme consciousness
A spiritual awakening that the Reality brings about!
That enlightens the soul and removes from its face
The thick veils of darkness.
Oh the Real, you have shown me all the ways leading to my reality
When fears swirl about me, and terror strikes
You're mirrored in my eyes of intellect with grace
And all the fear and terror goes off from my mind
And thus You pull the dervish out of the abyss of ignorance
The truth he comes to realize
That you are the eternal source and the essential truth
'I am from the fathomless ocean of light!'
The proclamation he makes without any fear!

150 I Look Out from Behind the Screens to See the Real

I look out from behind the screens to see the Real
The Real is showing up there in his enormous manifestation
The Real is looking at me with divine smile
The Real is the reality of my life
For I do not exist at all apart from the Real
The Real is the source of all existence!
All existence is nothing but manifestation of the Real!
The Gnostics when they perceive Divine Reality, declare:
La ilaha illa Hu!
La ilaha illa Hu!
Nothing exists except He!
I am not saying something strange to you
The Real speaks on my tongue:
'I am always one!'
'I am always unique!'
'Wherever you turn, there is the Face of Allah!' (Quran.)
A realized person does not see at the forms
But he sees rather in the forms
His eye of intellect sees all objects
In the world of manifestation
As the Names or Attributes of the Real
And his speech is all about the Real and His Absolute unity!

151 *A Feeling of Contentment and Ecstasy*

A feeling of contentment and ecstasy
When you hear the call from your God
Is a sure sign that your God is pleased with you
You must as such put your faith in deeds pleasing to God
Your desire to withdraw from everything that distracts your attention
When Allah has involved you in His constant zikr signifies
An evident sign of mercy from your God
Your desire for involvement with the people of knowledge means
That Allah wants to withdraw you from the people of ignorance
That is indeed a fulfillment of your high aspiration
To be in constant intimacy with the friends of God
Such is God's grace that He bestows
Upon whomever He wills
God is Possessor of Infinite Grace
Your Aspiration for awareness and enlightenment
Which springs from your brain to your heart is a hidden secret
That helps you break the walls of world's prison
And be like a free bird that soars up and up
A clear sign of Divine bounty on you
Give yourself a rest from roaming in wilderness!
When He whom you are seeking is not cut off from you
Don't you perceive that He is your essential truth
And that you do not live by yourself!

152 The Light of the Intellect Lets You See

The light of the intellect lets you see His nearness to you
The source of the intellect lets you see the signs in yourself and His universe
The eye of the intellect reveals to you the knowledge and wisdom
The ears of the intellect let you hear the tasbih from everything of his manifestation
The truth of the intellect lets you see His Absolute unity
The Truth tells you about His absolute existence through the intellect
Allah was and there was nothing besides Him!
Allah is and there is nothing besides Him!
Allah will be and there'll be nothing besides Him!

153 *As I Looked Through the Windows of My Eyes*

As I looked through the windows of my eyes
I found myself amazed in your melodious voice
I got filled with tremendous ecstasy
As I heard the most beautiful zikr—the king of zikr
That I truly desire.
The way you spoke to me with this mesmerizing voice
Together with your glaring light
That was truly awesome
This was more than just a casual event
This was truly your response to my prayers all the time
To call me back to my original place in heaven
That you have named as paradise
I always knew you'll call me back to the house of peace
To allow me be in perennial peace
I always knew you'll take me in your merciful lap
Under your graceful glances
This was an amazing dream!
I wish to see this dream till my end!
This is what I always have solemnly prayed for!
I thank You my GOD for your great blessing
For I couldn't ask for anything more.

154 *On the Path of Love*

On the path of Love we are neither masters nor the slaves
We are only dervishes going from one exhibition of our beloved to another exhibition
We go not with a begging bowel in our hands from door to door
We go with bouquets of flowers of love from one door to another
We are dervishes. Our beloved loves his beauty through our eyes
Our beloved hears his sweet melody through our ears
Nay, we are dervishes. We have nothing as our own
Our eyes, ears, and heart are of our beloved

155 The Real Bids the Brain to Generate Thoughts

The Real bids the brain to generate thoughts
The Real then begins to perform as You
The Real sees, hears, speaks, tastes, feels, acts, as You
You are not You separate from Real
Though You do not know
The thoughts are not Your thoughts
As the brain is not under your control
Thoughts are of Real!
These are commands through brain from Real to Real!
How can you stop your brain from thinking?
That is really impossible!
Only fools think of stopping their brain
The brain is under the control of Real
The stupid's do not know that a person is connected to
This world and to the other
Only through the brain
No action, no emotion, no passion is there before the thought is born
Think what will be you like
If you are without a functional brain
A lump of molded soil!
Just as the sunshine is a real event
And just the sun shines the world as it must
Thoughts will continue occurring in your brain

That is managed and administered by the Real
Thus the Real manifests itself as You
And lords over your world as You
You are not the cause of your thoughts
Rather it is the Real as originator of thoughts
Nothing other than Real can ever cause thoughts
It's all the flow of The Real!
It is all the manifestation of Real!
The Real is flowing as you right now and absolutely perfectly
If we only knew!
The thought is Real! The Thinker is Real! Brainless man is just a stone.

156 *If I Say That the Skies Have Opened Their Gates*

If I say that the skies have opened their gates
I mean I have found the way to be in eternal presence
If I say that I see the Light of the skies and the earth
I mean that my beloved has shown me His light
In his beautiful manifestation
If I say that the celestial melody is reverberating
In me and around
I mean that my sweetheart is speaking to me with a smile

157 *Hatif Whispered to Me*

Hatif whispered to me:
Let not the ignorant hear this secret
I'll tell you the secret way
That can lead you to the Truth:
Ignore the paths of others
Everyone has his own way
Ignore even the saints' steep trails
They are not living to lead you the way
Behold! Every saint has got his own way
Don't follow blindly!
Don't journey at all aimlessly!
Rip the veils from your face
You will know, you are the goal
You need not go elsewhere
Don't walk on the zigzag and crisscrossing roads
Walk on the straight path that goes from You to You
If the light is in your heart
You will find your way home (Rumi).

158 *I Had Heard That*

I had heard that,
having passed into the state of perfect annihilation
I would blaze my all thoughts—concerning Here and Hereafter
I thought it is the path to Thee, but
Ah! The reality is that actually
No person may ever be able to stop his brain becoming non-functional
None can ever draw near thee, save by Thy appointed ways!
My lord! I cannot live, without the thought of knowing You
Thy thought is overwhelming me: I cannot flee remembering thee
I had been given to believe that I can come to Thee
By stopping generating all thoughts save the thought about You
I for long wasted my time remaining busy with brooming away the thoughts from my mind
Instead of concentrating on You:
Lo! How can I sever every thought from my mind?
Only after death can brain stop functioning!
I can think of thee only as long as I have a living brain
That can flood me with thoughts to know and love thee!
Without thoughts man is but a clod of earth!

159 *At First, the Road of Love Seemed to Be*

At first, the road of love seemed to be
Leading me afar myself to God
I thought the road is very easy and short
I was under the impression that I'll reach
My God with meditation in the shortest time
After taking a few steps, I but found that
The road is long beyond my imagination
I got afraid that this road leads to nowhere
When I got frustrated at last, I found that
The road turned back to me, surprising me
I got to know that God was not far away from me
I realized that it was a journey
From me to me.

160 *They're Always Talking About Love, Love*

They're always talking about Love, Love
What Love is, they don't know
They are always discussing Heart, Heart
What the Heart is, they don't know
Within the heart of the lover soul is found
It isn't found anywhere outside
The lovers find the Truth in their own vast souls
What soul is, the hypocrites don't know
They pretend to be Gnostics, and pick up quarrels
Lot of questions! long empty talks! and fruitless discussions!
Their words are borrowed and deeds to show off their piety!
What is true and pure way, they don't know
They worship their ancestors, and pay obeisance on their mausoleums
They venerate the dead and do not seek knowledge
From the living sages
And from the people of knowledge the pearls of wisdom do not collect
What is awareness and enlightenment they don't know
They err in believing that their dead have got continued existence
And have ability to heal their ills
And in difficulty come to their succor
They seek help from non-Gods for easing their life and giving them fortunes
They believe that the dead in graves can intercede for them
'We serve thee and we seek help from thee', they don't know

Leaving all these absurdities, I became a true person
Through God's vast mercy I was forgiven and purged off the duality
I found absolute oneness of the Truth
In all manifestations
What the oneness is, they don't know
MyKoul proclaims the Truth is my reality
The Truth is everywhere if you are willing to see
When you come to know the Truth, there won't be any speech
What is the hidden truth of a human being
Mansur and Nasimi knew, but they don't know
Mansur was sent to gallows, while Nasimi was skinned alive.

161 *If You Have Died, How Can You Be My Savior?*

If you have died, how can you be my savior?
If you have died, how can you be my Imam?
If you have died, how can you rise from the dead?
If you have died, how can you hear my supplication?
If you have died, how can you help me?
If you have died, how can you harm me?
If you are still not born, why should I wait for you?
How can they hear, see, or speak
Who are in graves?
The dead cannot be equal to living!

162 *The Divine Eye*

Any eye filled with the vision of divine beauty
Can only see the creation as His manifestation
Any eye filled with the vision of differentiation
Would be deprived of the Beauty of Oneness

163 *The River Has Been Looking for You*

The river has been looking for you
Since eternity
It was looking for you when you were still unborn
It was connected to you inside the mother's womb
Through umbilical cord
It appeared in your mother's breasts to quench
Your thirst and hunger
Many a time you run for water in the ten directions
You don't know that the ancient river is within you
Woe unto you! You looked for water outside you
I recognized you on so many different dry wells
Looking for water
What are you doing, my darling?
I have been with you since the Time's beginning
When in the remote past, of my spirit I blew into you
You are still wandering for water far away from me
I have been calling you by your name in your each search
Come unto me, I am near to you
More near than your jugular vein!
Be confident that even though you have lost your way to me
You will finally find a way back to me
To have at source enough of the water of life
Open up the lids on your eyes
I manifest myself right beside you
I am travelling with you, believe me
On the road you are treading to look for me

But you are still looking at others for guidance

As if I were not with you

You cannot see the connection between you and me

For you have become blind to see the truth

The old covenant with me you have forgotten

How can you enter into a new covenant with me?

You do not recognize me for your mind is caught up in mirages

Come on! I am in you! I am by you! I am around you!

All your lifetime, you must get the water of life from me.

164 Let Me Enjoy Walking Together with Nature

Let me enjoy walking together with nature!
Let me sit together with nature for a longtime
At the foot of old pine trees!
Let me stand side by side with nature
In silence for hours, listening to
The sound of the wind softly calling me!
Let me watch at the white clouds floating over my head!
Let me pick up fallen blossom petals
And make a beautiful wreathe!
Let me enjoy beautiful autumn
Looking at the burning chinars of my land!
Let me go alone through forests deep in snow!
But wherever I go I always will remember
My ancient home
Where I lived near to my lord in peace
Let me hear the big bells from morning to evening
That sound to wake up the sleeping self.

165 *My Yearning for Allah Grows Acute*

My yearning for Allah grows acute with every passing day
My heart gets obsessed with his zikr with every passing day
My longing for Allah gets stronger with every passing day
My eyes roll up, high and higher, with every passing day
My eyes fix their glances without waver at His beautiful manifestation
His shining face appears to me as I vision His colorful manifestation
My joy knows no bounds as I smell the fragrance of His beautiful flowers
I perceive His oneness with the eye of my intellect as I sight His visions
Wheresoever I turn to, His face shines like the full moon
A brilliant light radiates from His suns of His manifestation
That illuminate my black eyes, and give me enlightenment
I am sure His light is the essence of my life, and of the entire universe
The truth is that it is the glory of God from which all other glories emanate
Allah is the Light of the heavens and the earth
Light upon Light!
Allah guides to His Light whom He wills.

166 The Sage Says

Knowledge is beauty
Ignorance is ugliness
Wisdom is virtue, folly is evil
Recognize virtue, avoid evil
'Is' is known after knowing 'Is not'
The success is born from failure
The ease is born from difficulty
Light is defined by darkness
The sage understands this with meditation
He always adds to his knowledge
And improves his wisdom.

167 *Woe Unto You!*

Woe unto you!
You're looking at the sun
See at its reflection
In the clear pond of water
You're seeking to know
The soul of the world
Come to your own self
Seek your own essence
Your True self, that is
Present in you and in every place
Now that you've known your True self
You'll find the hidden truth:
He has made His home in your heart!
When you find him in your home
You'll not seek Him outside
In other homes
He who abides in your home
Abides in every home.

168 *At Last, I Am Free*

At last, I am free
At last am I a faqir free!
No more am I tied to any order
I am free from the taqlid of five Imams
Hanbali, Hanfi, Maliki, Shaafi and Jeffrey
On my heart's writing pad
I write only what my God lets me know
No more am I bound to the sages
Sleeping in graves
They did not and cannot
Teach me an alphabet or a word
No more do I read volumes of philosophies and poetry
I weave my own thoughts on poems' loom
No more delusion! No more illusion!
I sit now in the shade of my own tree
Meditating thus, I am happy, and free.

169 *Wondrous is the Mercy of God!*

Wondrous is the mercy of God!
His mercy has graced the thorns with roses!
His mercy manifests in man and the universe!
His mercy is evident in His beautiful manifestation!
It matters not whether His mercy is thanked by any person
I pray for His special mercy
For giving me to drink the wine of love
Oh friend! What a great bliss lies in wine of love!
The wine of love can never cause derangement
The wine of love causes awareness and enlightenment
The wine of love sprouts from beneath knowledge and wisdom
One cannot get knowledge of divine mysteries by reading books
The benefits of the wine of Love
Can never be described in words
I have never understood real love from books
For it cannot be transmitted in words
The wine of Love runs through the veins of lover's heart
Oh God! Grant me the gift of Your wine of love
Oh God! I long to live in Your garden of love
Oh God! In Your books write not my name
As a person away from you
Oh God! You know I always try to be in your presence
Nobody can question my true and sincere love
Oh God! You directly offer me the wine of love to drink
Oh God! Your presence is in everything and everywhere

Why should i feel separated from your presence

You shower Your immense mercies upon me.

170 Man! You Must Have Infinite Love for All Humankind

Man! you must have infinite love for all humankind
You must make no distinction in love
Between the blessed soul and unblessed soul
Just as God loves even the lowliest of the souls
That are lost to the evil and devil
Man! rejoice that God dwells in your heart
Still more highly rejoice that your soul is from God
Your heart is made in eternity to be God's abode
The original home of your soul is God
Who is manifested in you and all the things
So man! you must be in the image of God
Who is most beneficent, most merciful, all-love.

171 *The Paradise Has No One Gate*

The paradise has no one gate
There are thousands of ways going to it
If you walk on the road of love
That is the shortest and straight
But you can't take with you any guide
No savior! No intercessor!
You have to walk to the paradise alone
The abode of enduring peace and comfort!
As God says:
No soul knows what comfort
Has been concealed from them
As a reward for what they did (to know Him).

172 *Happiness is Not Enduring*

Happiness is not enduring and sorrow continues to be long
Why happiness is short-lived and sorrow continues to be long?
Because men do not live of, or for, equanimous and peaceful life
This is why they are happy just for a short while and unhappy for long
Therefore the sage makes peace and tranquility his way of life
And yet peace is to be found only in pure and sincere love
At the center of our being is love; pure and sincere love!
Love is the source of enduring happiness—spiritual ecstasies
Love removes all agonies and wards off all miseries
We must recover and protect this invaluable treasure
Love is the song of the soul, singing to God in rhythmic tones
Love is the surrender to the beloved's call of 'Come near unto Me'
Love is the elixir of life, reviving dead souls to life
Love is the ineffable, silent call of the heart to live in divine
Love is the fragrance of the divine rose of ecstasies
Love is like the Hamsa that flies to the Cosmic Home
To gaze with looks of wonderment on divine manifestation
And to proclaim through silent speech:
God manifests His beauty to Himself—as the prophet says:
Indeed God is beautiful, and He loves His own beauty.

173 *My Soul is Eternal Music*

My soul is eternal music that plays behind the veils
Only the glorious tunes of music I constantly hear
The eternal music that I hear initiate me into God
I am a holy listener of God's song of love from eternity
When I hear the sound of musical streams running into my heart
I fall into deep intoxication as I drink the wine of music
What can I say of my ecstasy that I feel
When hearing with my eyes the song of love
Only the mystics inebriated with the wine of love
Experience such an ecstasy
The soul's music produces light most bright
That burns away the darkness
Only the glorious song of love the lovers of God as such hear!
The song of love, I swear, initiated me into God
Only His glorious song of love do I have
As my precious gift from God!

174 *If I Would Have It So*

If I would have it so
I will never end my hearing your song of love
If it sets my heart's piano well-tuned
I will set my eyes fixed on your beautiful manifestation
If I understand the road does not go to your home but to Zulmat
I will surely abandon this road and take another road
That goes straight to your home, the abode of Love
If it confuses me and distracts me from your perpetual remembrance
I will shun pursuing worldly pleasures and charmful things
If it takes me away from myself and fuses me to your oneness
I will keep rowing my boat in the ocean of oneness.

175 *The Mystery That Can Be Known*

The mystery that can be known
Is not the hidden and true mystery
The mystery that can be named
Is not the hidden and real mystery
He who is the hidden mystery
Is the Originator of seven heavens and earth
And whatever is in between them
His manifestations can be given a name
But He is nameless: who can give him any name?
He begets not, nor is he begotten!
He is the creator of all things!
He is his own manifestation!
Nothing is like or unlike him!
How can you compare him with anything
And give him a name?
He is the Exalted, and exists eternally!
He is not a body, Jawhar, or accident!
He is not on a place or in a place!
Always He is a mystery that we must try to find!
Through meditation and contemplation, we can find but
That He is only the hidden mystery!
No one is able to find His deep mystery!
If we desire to know His mystery a little
We can see it within us
But not in its entirety!
Its outer fringe is all that we can see!

Under all circumstances, He is really the same mystery!

Mystery! Mystery! Mystery! Mystery!

As we understand some aspect of this mystery

We give it a name

So we find different names given by mystics to the same reality!

The nameless still remains a hidden mystery!

His manifestations too are his mysteries

Together we call them God—the Hidden Mystery!

You are the Mystery! The Universe is mystery!

The Truth is the mystery of everything!

So I call the Truth by the name of the Hidden mystery.

176 We Must Hear and Speak What is Truth

We must hear and speak what is truth
Hearing the truth fills the mind with truth
That comes on the tongue as the true speech
We speak a lie because we hear and see lie
That pollutes our mind
And so naturally evil words come on our tongues
We must be lovers of the Truth
Hearing, seeing, thinking, and speaking truth
Is the true religion
We must love the Truth and be afraid of untruth
We must hear and see truth that goes to our mind
And grows true thoughts there, and
A true speech on our tongues is born
He who has this secret known
He must peep into his heart: the temple of the Truth!
Where there is peace, and tranquility and love
We must take precautions in the darkness
And go inside to see for ourselves the Truth
Why this wild search afar, outside our hearts?
The Truth is in every heart: the essence of every soul
If it is in the heart of Saint and sage, why not in you?
(Says MyKoul) the Truth is not far from any soul
Without the presence of the Truth, man cannot be the vicegerent of God!
That explains the secret between Adam and God

But everyone has not the eye to see the Truth

I must say what comes to my heart from the Truth.

177 All in the World Do Not Know the Beauty of the Beautiful

All in the world do not know the beauty of the beautiful
Though the prophet says:
Allah is beautiful, and He loves His own beauty
In understanding this way, the lovers have no idea of what ugliness is
They all know the beauty of the beautiful, in all colorful dresses
In knowing this way, they have the clear idea of what the divine is
So it is the appreciation and non-appreciation of beauty
That give birth to the idea of the other
Light and darkness are both the necessary beauties manifested by the beautiful
Spring and winter, summer and fall, are necessary beauties of the beautiful
His is the unmatchable beauty!
He is the peerless and unequalled!
The Gnostics of his unique divinity
Do not compare and contrast
The ideas of differentiation—high and low—arise
From the contrast and comparison
The things that are apparently different
Are components of one whole
Just as the musical notes and tones become
Harmonious and produce sweet melody
Through the relation of one with another

As such, the sages understand one single beautiful reality
Manifested through multifarious beauties
They do not make any differentiation
They listen from the divine without the use of speech
That all things spring up from Him
And there is no one which of its own can show itself
There exists no one but He, everything is his manifestation
The work of His manifestation is never accomplished
He does not take rest on the sixth day!
On every time, He is bringing about a new manifestation
He himself is complete and perfect
No one can see him except his manifestations!
Tis what makes me believe:
God is beautiful and He loves His own beauty.

178 By What Name Do I Have to Call You?

By what name do I have to call you?
Certainly you are not known to any person in your entirety
Who can choose a befitting name for you?
In the sense that the planets have been given names
Just walking around, and finding your beautiful manifestation!
A secret of curiosity to Gnostics, philosophers, and prophets!
But you are too clearly manifested through everything and everyone
You are the secret of all beauties around
And you are the truth of every soul
To say much about you is impossible
You are our wonder, beauty around
You are smiling to us through every beautiful face
In your presence we never feel lonely and alone
We find you with us wherever we are
You never put us off
As we realize your presence in us and around
All the curtains between get off
That the shortest way is the most efficient way
That is your all-around beauty
There is light and music sweet in your beautiful manifestation
What a great mystery of divine presence!
Come my friends and see it!
Come not near to any thought or sight undivine
Come but near to divine beauty

But if you don't still see him in dresses beautiful

Grant that He sees you constantly.

179 Sincere Lovers are Ever Intoxicated by the Music of Love

Sincere Lovers are ever intoxicated by the music of Love
A mystic silence is needed to hear this melody
The musician veiled in the rhythmic tunes seeks
Pure love from the hearers of his Song of love
What does He whisper to His lovers?
Only Earnest love!
Love is the subject of their wordless conversation
In Love no longer 'separation' and 'union' exist
For? when you know the absolute unity
You will not be obsessed by the fear of distance
Nor will you crave for nearness to Him
For He is whole:
Everything and everyone is His manifestation
For believers in Absolute Unity
There is no room for I, You, and He
Thought of duality or multiplicity is nothing
But ignorance about reality
Draw aside all the veils from the Truth
Then, in the Temple of love, you will love the formless
In his beautiful manifestations
He who would know the secret of His manifestation
Will find the secret of His presence
In his self and all other things in the universe
As the Qur'an says:

'And on the earth are signs for those
Who have faith with certitude
And also in your own selves are Signs
Of Divine Omnipotence, Grandeur, and Wisdom
Will you not then see with your inward sight?

180 Ask Those Who Have Got Knowledge Divine

Ask those who have got knowledge divine
What's this thinking person
The amalgam of soul and body?
By what command he inhales and exhales?
What voice in rhythmic tones he hears?
They will tell you in the words of the Quran:
The Spirit comes by command of my Lord
Of knowledge it is only a little
That is communicated to you
The Lord sits on the throne
And issues the command
Who is the King on the throne, and
Who are you that is commanded?
Give thanks to your creator
Created you when nothing existed
From His command: Kun Fayakun!
And since we are actually nothing
Whose are all these powers and riches
That we possess?
MyKoul knows that he is nothing
But the command of God
That He inspires in him since the First day
The world won't last forever

But my Truth will remain

What are You, my Lord? What am I?

181 *Glory Be to Muhammad*

The word of wisdom sent down from Truth
He revealed to us
The sublime knowledge of Truth!
He explained to us great mysteries
About God and His beautiful manifestation
And we swam and dived into the Ocean of One
Glory be to Muhammad!
Beyond the bare hills, arid lands and deserts
Of delusion, illusion, and ignorance
He guided us like a shepherd guides his flocks
To graze in grasslands, meadows and moors
Under his guidance, we learnt to live
Romantic, joyful, and peaceful divinely life
Glory be to Muhammad!
We were like dry and lifeless plants in winter
He moistened us with the water of life
We grew big and became green plants
We recognized our true self
And came back to life after we were dead
Glory be to Muhammad!
To whatever lands we belonged
To whatever races and languages we belonged
He joined us together into one humanity
He taught us the meanings taught to him by God
All the 6666 verses in the Qur'an
And nothing did he hide from us

Glory be to Muhammad!
He came here at the end of long trail of prophets
To advise us to live in peace and harmony
Let's be as members of universal brotherhood
And not live as strangers to one another
Let's live under his banner, and follow his golden teachings
Glory be to Muhammad!
He showed us the straight road to God, and said:
He is most near to you—wherever you are, He is with you
Don't panic, don't lose hope, and don't fight with each other
Then you can live a peaceful life, without any strife
Glory be to Muhammad!
It's the same truth with you and me—the universal message!
Nothing reduces stress like the presence of the wise Shepherd!
When you are living in close connection to Muhammad
You can find the road to God, and will not get lost.
Glory be to Muhammad!

182 Arifs' Hearts with Knowledge and Wisdom

Arifs' hearts with knowledge and wisdom are blest
Arifs' eyes with divinely sight are blest
Arifs' ears hear in the audience hall divine
The word of Allah: there is no deity but Hu
Arifs' intellect perceives what rationalists perceive not
Arifs' tongues deliver divine speech of secrets
Arifs do not speak words of delusion, and myths
Arifs wordless conversation with God
Is beyond the recording angels' pen
Arifs fly with the wings of hope and fear
To divine presence getting detached from attributes undivine
Arifs are inheritors of the sciences of hidden secret
Rather than all lore of nonsense and falsehood
Arifs speak about the great signs of God
And nullify impostors' all claims.

183 *Midnight*

Midnight—no light, no sound
Midnight—no birds singing
Midnight—no insects singing
Midnight—sitting still
Midnight—empty mind
Midnight—Heart awake
Midnight—Soul in zikr
Midnight—Hearing zikr
Midnight—in the mid-prayer
Midnight—only Allah: with me
Midnight—whole life be as if midnight.

184 I Will Rise Again in the Life Hereafter

I will rise again in the life Hereafter
My Love will welcome me with a gentle smile
About the things that remained undone or half done
I will ask my Love, Let you give me one more life
He will offer me life in paradise
He will not turn me away
He will not consign me to scorching flames of fire
He will allow me to continue to be in His presence
I will persist in the state of peace and equanimity
My holy dream will not be broken abruptly there
As it amazingly breaks sometimes here
In presence with my Love there
My heart will be in perpetual ecstasy
Hearing sweet melody, and seeing light upon light
There the fountain of love will never dry
In that everlasting Garden, I will hear no empty talk
Countless springs will flow there
There will be thrones of happiness raised high
And goblets of wine of love placed ready
This is what God has promised me in His Book.

185 *In the Path of Love*

In the path of love
The eye must cease to see, the ear must cease to hear
The heart must cease to perceive
Save of Him, and about Him
Be a traveler on His path
On this journey
You will go beyond yourself
And know the ultimate truth
The goal finally achieved!

186 Once I Was Not Here

Once I was not here
Not in this form!
There has come upon me
A period of time
When I was nothing!
But now I am a man:
The most beautiful thing!
The most perfect being!
If there's really a secret
It is only me!
It is only me!
If the truth can be known
And encompassed at all
It could only be known by man
Not by any other being
Man, the super creation of God!
Whom God gave life by his own spirit
That very spirit whispers
To people of knowledge and wisdom:
'If anybody could be in God's image
It could only be you
Man, you have nothing of your own
Neither body nor soul!
If I had any body, if I had any soul
Then, without question, it could only be you.

But, I have neither body, nor soul

I am what I am! '

187 *As the Night of Darkness Was Ending*

As the night of darkness was ending
And the sunlight came in from all sides
My heart, mind, and soul came out of dreaming
My eyes woke from deep sleep
Then, the dawn sought to greet me with light
The morning birds greeted me with sweet music
As if master musician in his hands held the lute
And moved his fingers skillfully over the strings
Where are You Master musician, who keeps my heart awake?
Every moment sweet lute sound is coming from You
So that I feel myself no longer separate from You.
The lute sound is echoing from every side—sweet music of love!
If you reflect on this mysterious lute
You will see that it says: Come to me! Come to me!
Listen O friend, God is calling you from every side!
Your lord is saying: Call upon me, I will respond to your call
He invites you to the Home of Peace [i.e., Paradise]
He guides whom He wills to the straight path—that goes to Him.

188 *The Hidden Mystery!*

The Hidden Mystery!
It speaks to me in the silence of the night!
It speaks to me through the tweets of morning birds!
It speaks to me through the noising birds in the evening!
It speaks to me through the twinkling and winking stars!
It speaks to me through the shining moon on the Full-moon night!
It speaks to me through the smiling sun at dawn!
It speaks to me on a cloudy night
When moon and stars play Hide and Seek!
It speaks to me on a hot summer day
When nobody dares to look at the sun's face!
And do you know what words it whispers into my ear?
It says to me confidently:
'I am Light: heaven and earth cannot contain me
I am Light: no eye can see me
I am the Wondrous Phoenix
Whom nobody has seen
I am hidden mystery:
I through my creativity manifest my beauty
I speak with every tongue!
I listen with all ears!
I see with all eyes!
My tongue, my ears, and my eyes are you!
Since in all the world only I exist
No likeness or unlikeness can be found of me.'

My Lord's whisper has done more for me

Than any scripture I will ever study!

189 *Nightingale!*

O nightingale!
Hidden behind the bushes and groves thick!
O sweet-voiced Beauty, nightingale!
Come with the sweet melodies
Make me fused to your ecstasies
Make me witness your unequalled Beauty
Let hundreds of your angels in the Heaven
Let Hundreds of your friends in the earth
Known and unknown
With radiant faces and brightful eyes
Be witness to my sincere love for you
Your love makes everyone sing and dance
Men, women, all celebrate festively
When you unveil to them your beauty
Because of your merciful bounties, please
Save us from worldly griefs and agonies
Because world for your lovers is
Like a dragon of cruelty
O beautifully-voiced Sweetheart!
Cool my ears and eyes, soul and heart
With Your sweet, soft melodies
With Your mercy, allow me entry please
In the land of your Presence
Please blow your breath in my ear
So that I hear the secret melodies
That your chosen lovers hear from eternity.

190 Beloved, Whose Love Gives His Birds Wings

O Beloved, whose Love gives His birds wings
To fly in the sky of spiritual ecstasies
And makes them soar higher and higher
To reach your throne, and circumambulate
Through Your magnetic pull of Love
'I can't detach myself from your strong hold.'
Your secrets full with meanings deep
Behind forms and shapes are seen
Every moment by your lovers true
By the eyes you have given them to see
Some of your hidden things, by your leave
Hearts of your lovers have turned into eyes
That see You as the causeless cause of all creation
O beloved, I cannot call You by any particular name
The names of all the things are truly your names
O Beloved, who has seen you with his fleshy eyes?
But you split open the hearts of your lovers to reveal them
A little of knowledge
To those who strive in You (to know you)
You certainly (through granting them knowledge and wisdom)
Guide them to your Paths to know your omnipresence and omniscience.

191 *If You Can Take Care of Elementary Needs*

If you can take care of elementary needs, do so!
But when you're living at home with your God
You should not sew the world together with desires
Nor should you tear it apart with renunciation
When you are at home with God
Existence and non-existence itself is illusion
All that is in you and out of you, is one!
When you are at home with God
Whether you are a Zahid or Sufi
Such a superfluous categorisation disappears
When you are at home with God
Whether you are a Muslim or a Kafir
No such distinction remains
When you are at home with God
You have got what you have sought:
The essence beyond any cause!
Be more like the servant who owns nothing
But is satisfied with whatever he gets from his master
He does not feel appetite for having more and more
He does no crave for anything from anyone except from God
He does not grieve or fear anyone other than God.

192 *Being Humble is Right for You*

Being humble is right for you
Don't brag and boast about yourself
Do not assert your superiority over others
Stop behaving like a wolf
Terrifying the people around you
Be always soft and gentle—down to earth!
But burst like a lion from the cage
When speaking for the defense of truth
Thus admonished my murshid, M. Rajab, to me.

193 *You Are Not Far from Your Friend*

You are not far from your friend
He is nearer to you than your jugular vein
But you must set out along the Road of love
The Road of Love passes through you
The Road of Love consists of neither words nor songs: only delusion can come from these
And never any lasting peace and equanimity!
Love and peace are the words of the traveler
Who treads the Road of Love in silence
When he speaks he speaks from awareness
And when he is silent, he is engrossed in contemplation
Gazing upon the light divine and hearing the music divine
Thus advised my murshid, M. Rajab, to me.

194 When the Truth of Oneness Manifested on Me

When the truth of Oneness manifested on me, I saw
That the Truth is beyond the pronouns of 'I', 'You', and 'He'
When my heart's eye opened
I was freed from counting and differentiation
Nothing other than the One did I see!
I was freed from duality and multiplicity!
When I came to understand the Absolute Unity
I felt I have seen all that there was to be seen
There's no duality in the world of love:
What's all this talk of 'I' 'you' and 'He'?
All letters are essentially the letter Alif shaped differently!

195 *Ironic, the Most Invaluable Thing*

Ironic, the most invaluable thing that
We do not appreciate and venerate is life
So beautiful is Life but we kill it's beauty day in and day out
We cannot get this life back once death takes us away
Let us say "yes" to Life
Life will say "yes" back to us
To live after death this is the golden key
Let us Live our life to achieve Eternity:
The Life's purpose
Let us use our wings to soar high and higher
And touch the shining stars
That enlighten us with knowledge and wisdom
We can do it, that is sure!
God in eternity has given us wings to fly in His skies
Those who glow with the light of knowledge and wisdom
Are freed from ignorance, illusion, and delusion
They are the true friends of Allah 'Behold! verily on the friends of Allah
There is no fear, nor shall they grieve'
But, they who are unenlightened and unaware
Only add knots to their yarn-ball of life.

196 *Glorify My Beloved's Name*

Glorify my beloved's Name all things in the universe
Let me hear hymns of praise in silence
And sweet music from Heaven coming
In the innermost chamber of my heart
Let my love, yearnings and longings be reflected
In my prayers and poems
The flowers of the rose garden of the world
Lose their glory and beauty after some time
But my Love's beauty is eternal, that never wanes
O' Cupbearer! Give me to drink cups of Prem-Ras (the wine of love)
Which will keep me intoxicated forever
My Love, you are my heart's throbbing
Let my dreams, visions and hopes
Be filled with your glory and your remembrance
O Lord! Open my inner eye to see your presence
In your charming and beautiful creation
I know you are hidden behind your own curtains
If you do not lift curtains on your face
I will never be able to see unity in diversity
I will never be able to come out of polemical debates about you.

197 *Now as the Morning Sun Swings Down*

Now as the morning sun swings down
And the sunlight encloses the vast world
I too enter the hour when my inside is
Filled with the light and music of love
I see, He's inside me
Just as the sun we see in the tumbler of still water
Who says He keeps His distance from His Lover?
Don't be under such terrible illusion
He stands before your eyes
But is dressed in many guises
His most sublime and splendid image but are you!
He, verily, is the Perfection of
Love, Peace and Beauty!
When you get to know these attributes three
You will know the hidden meaning of Alif Laam Meem
Let you gaze upon the Truth with your Heart's eye
Because the hidden the truth, if you want to see
You can vividly see in yourself
You are the best creation and the manifestation of the Lord
Be not under any delusion!
The same truth that is expressed in the world of varied forms!
Every form is certainly the creation and manifestation of the Truth.

198 *The True Force Divine Moves*

The true force divine moves
The vast world of creation:
Radiating light, glowing life, and deep secrets
Consider, man, whither thy soul is going?
Behold the way that goes through your heart to the Lord
Behold, how His Light shows the way to Himself
And know that His Light crushes all darkness
For from the depths of darkness
God leads into light: The Truth!
The Truth is the final reality—everlasting!
The untruth cannot lastingly prevail!
O man, abandon falsehood, strive on
Like falcons flying toward the skies
Discovering: Immortality! Eternity!
How canst thou call real what is ephemeral?
THERE has been an endless span of time
Before man came to this world
Then God created man out of a drop of sperm intermingled
And made him a being endowed with
Hearing and sight
To show him the way to Himself
It rests with man to journey through space and time
Towards the truth
Blessed is He whom the truth has kissed
On his eyes and ears
He sees God's light in all the things of the world

He hears God's word resonating from all the things
He, therefore, loves beauty
And says nothing is ugly
He loves the beautiful, because it tells of God
God is beautiful and He loves His own beauty!
The people with eyes see His beauty
Spread out in the whole of universe
Because it is profound and never dies!

199 *The Eternal Mysteries*

The eternal mysteries
Following All-wisdom's lead
Brought forth the human consciousness
As the living proof of the divine providence
As long as
He hadn't blown into man
Of his Spirit (consciousness)
His power, His all-countless attributes
Were unknown to man
Even so Man cannot measure
The full depths of His splendor.

200 Till the End of My Sojourn in This World

Till the end of my sojourn in this world
Let me always stay occupied with your Zikr
When I come to hear your fragrant speech
I believe you'll come out to see me
Showering your sunshine on me
My love, come! I'm waiting on your door
For one smile from you
And I'll my heart upon the burning altar of your love throw
When you come to rule my heart
I will be freed from the obsession of Salvation and damnation
I will be freed from the botheration of
Belief and disbelief.
When I go beyond myself, I will see finally the reality.

About The Author

Dr. Mohammad Younus Koul, known by his pen name MyKoul, embarks on his poetic journey with the publication of his debut collection, The Divine Whispers: Songs of the Truth. This first volume in a planned series features two hundred poems and offers a profound exploration of spiritual awakening and divine reality. Dr. Koul's perspective is shaped by his academic achievements and spiritual experiences.

Academic and Professional Background

Dr. Koul holds an M.Com. from the erstwhile Jammu and Kashmir University, an M.A. in Economics from The University of Kashmir, Srinagar, and a Ph.D. in International Marketing from Panjab University, Chandigarh. He served as the Director of the Department of Management Studies at Islamia College, University of Kashmir, until his retirement in 2006. His distinguished academic career informs his reflective and insightful writing style.

Personal and Spiritual Journey

Dr. Koul's life was deeply impacted by the tragic loss of his father and brother in Dal Lake during his youth. Raised by his mother and elder brothers, he is rooted in his family's spiritual heritage, tracing back to Baba Usman

Koul, a caliph of Sheikh Hamza Makhdoom. At 25, he met the mystic Mohammad Rajab Gunna of Gagribal, Dalgate, who became his spiritual guide and initiated him as a disciple in 1975. This spiritual journey has been a cornerstone of his life.

The Emergence of Poetry

In 2018, following cataract surgery, Dr. Koul began writing poetry despite having no prior experience. He regards this as a divine gift that sparked his creative expression, leading to the creation of over 3,000 poems focused on divine love, reality, truth, and the human-divine connection. The Divine Whispers is the first volume in a series that will encompass this extensive body of work.

The Divine Whispers: A Journey of Self-Discovery

The Divine Whispers: Songs of the Truth explores themes of love, enlightenment, and the quest for truth. Through introspection and mystical experiences, Dr. Koul's poetry captures the relationship between the human soul and the divine, highlighting moments of revelation and the beauty of the natural world. His work serves as a spiritual guide, inspiring readers to reflect on their path toward enlightenment.

Acknowledgement

I extend my deepest gratitude to the Divine for guiding me on this journey of spiritual exploration. Without infinite blessings and grace, this book would not have been possible.

To my beloved wife, Ms. Shahzada, whose unwavering support, love, and faith have been the bedrock of my spiritual journey. Your presence in my life is an invaluable gift, and I am eternally grateful for your companionship.

To my cherished children, whose love and encouragement have inspired me to reach my potential. Your belief in me has been a constant source of strength and motivation.

I am also grateful to my nephews, Dr. Aabid Mustafa Koul and Abdul Manan Koul, who were instrumental in persuading me to share my collection with a wider audience.

I am profoundly indebted to my spiritual guide, Mohammad Rajab Gunna of Gagribal, Dalgate, Srinagar, whose wisdom and teachings have illuminated my path. Your guidance has been crucial in shaping my understanding of the divine.

My heartfelt thanks to my lifelong friend, M. Faroque Khateeb, and to all my friends and companions who have shared in this spiritual journey. Your friendship and camaraderie have enriched my life beyond measure.

Finally, a special note of appreciation to Basit Wani for his valuable support in compiling this book.

www.ingramcontent.com/pod-product-compliance
Ingram Content Group UK Ltd.
Pitfield, Milton Keynes, MK11 3LW, UK
UKHW020050200726
13845UKWH00055B/723

9 789334 087451